Praise for
"Tie-Ins For Life"

I have had the distinct honor to be Joe Shusko's friend for over 35 years. Over those years I have seen Joe lead, mentor, and motivate those around him like few others could. His "Tie-ins for Life" is a compilation of Joe's insights learned through leading by example and living by a strict moral compass. The stories he relates are about a universal truth: live a principled life to its fullest, share your acquired wisdom, and you will change the world. While too often today short shrift is given to ethics, honor, and integrity, this book is a shining example for everyone in every walk of life of what those values mean and why they are so important. I guarantee you will be changed and inspired by Joe's stories!

~ *Pat Marshall, Chief New Medias Officer, Yellowbook*

Joe Shusko's book, "Tie-ins for Life," is a gem of a book. Why? Because it comes from the heart. I have heard Joe tell these stories in front of many audiences, from battle-hardened Marines to skeptical civilians and everyone in between. The reaction? "These stories are great!" And they are great, because Joe has found the secret to teaching moral values: tell stories that touch

people – not only in their heads – but deep in their hearts and consciences.

Today it seems that everyone is talking about "core values." But, mission statements and bullet points don't activate the innate moral sense that lies within almost all of us. These stories do. Read one tonight – to yourself, to your children – before you go to bed. You'll sleep very well.

~ Jack Hoban President of Resolution Group International

This collection is needed more now than ever before, because truth and integrity are often found "missing in action." This compilation of "Tie ins for Life" is typical for Joseph Shusko because his success cannot be measured by the size of his wallet, but the size of his heart and commitment to his country and his fellow man. He is a Marine's Marine. Any modicum of success that Joe Shusko has experienced has been because of his unwavering commitment to excellence, with honor, and being the very best. Joe Shusko is in a league of his own, not only because he has the mental strength and moral courage to persist, but also because he has adopted the guiding principles espoused in this collection of "Tie ins for Life." What an awesome way to start and finish your day.

~ Phil Wilson, Colonel, US Marine Corps (Ret)

Tie-Ins for Life

Compiled by Joseph C. Shusko

ISBN ISBN-13: 978-1466395565

ISBN-10: 1466395567

Edition Notice (2nd)
Date of publication (2015)

RGI
Media and Publications
on the web at www.rgi.co
Post Office Box 652
Spring Lake, NJ 07762 USA

Table of Contents

Acknowledgements

Most of the stories and quotes in this book were compiled and edited by me from many different places, sources and people over a number of years. They came from family, friends, fellow Marines, books, magazines and the Internet. I have tried mightily to give credit where credit is due, but the source of many of these stories are unknown. I have made every effort to acknowledge the source of each story. If you read a story herein that you believe should be credited to you, please let me know and I will make the correction in any new edition or reprinting of this book. That said, I want to thank everyone who contributed to this venture. Your stories, the quotes and the tie-ins, have considerably improved this document and my life, and I sincerely apologize for any unintentional errors or omissions.

To Kadie, Joe, Kristin and Emmie with all my love and affection. Thank you for being the ones closest to me who sparked my light and inspired me to complete this collection. Thank you also for being the wonderful guinea pigs of my tie-ins over the years.

I would be remiss if I did not thank the thousands upon thousands of ethical warriors, United States Marines; I have given a number of these tie-ins to, and anyone who would listen to me pontificate. Thank you for believing in me and being the Protectors and Defenders of our Great Constitution. You truly are our Ethical Protectors and Defenders of this great Nation.

Semper Fidelis!
~ Joe Marine

i

Foreword

Joe enjoys the reputation as one who possesses a keen desire to impact others and help them grow. Blessed with over a decade of direct interaction with the Corps' most important officer (the 2nd Lieutenant), Joe has worked assiduously to craft tools that enable and inspire young leaders to examine themselves mentally, emotionally, physically and spiritually.

Young leaders learn more and grow faster by connecting with those who have paid the price and set the pace for others in difficult missions. Joe helps others make this connection through the medium of storytelling, providing a compendium of "tie-ins," rich with salient lessons associated with taking responsibility for others.

This small collection provides any leader an interesting and enjoyable study; however, the power of these vignettes lies in the imagination and ability of the leader to utilize them to both amplify and spawn meaningful dialogue on key issues at hand. I congratulate Joe on bringing these small but powerful messages together to serve as a tool for others to improve their own lives and those of others they are privileged to lead. I think that the lessons within these pages rank as especially relevant for the young, combat leader who undoubtedly "does the heavy lifting" in our country's current battles, as honor, courage and commitment have NEVER been more important. May these stories be "arrows in the quiver" of those who prepare for the most sacred responsibility of life: the honor of leading others in worthy pursuits.

~ *MajGen Thomas Jones, USMC (Ret)*

Introduction

This book is an "update" to the original Tie-ins book released in 2011. I have always wanted to add a mentoring piece to the tie-ins I have been using for years. This updated edition is a collection of short stories and quotes to those looking for personal motivation and for words to express themselves when seeking to encourage others.

I have been collecting these special little stories that have made a difference in my life for many years and I call them tie-ins. These tie-ins act as a guiding light to bring out the values that reside in all our hearts and reinforce an ethical lifestyle.

I'd again like to personally thank the many, many wonderful people in my life who have taken the time to send me the tie-ins included in this book. As you grow to be the very best mentor/leader you can be, I wish you well.

Each story requires minimal time to share with the maximum reward in remembering why we have been put on this earth in the first place.

This humble little book is designed for people of all ages who love to mentor and who make a positive difference in lives of others. I love calling these people givers of life. Givers of life are those you look up to as father and mother figures, teachers and scholars, coaches and counselors; they are people you'd love to be like or, simply put, mentors!

Mentoring has always been a big part of my life. It starts with the "two most favorite words in the English language" that I learned from my mentor, Major General Tom Jones: "Genuine Concern." Mentoring requires a genuine concern of truly being there for someone 24 hours a day, seven days a week, 365 days a year in both their personal and professional lives.

Mentoring and these tie-ins have helped me through a number of challenges in my life. I have also used these tie-ins to help others in good times and through bad times.

These tie-ins are linked to our foundation: values as good people who believe God created all men equal. I just wish it were practiced more. Our world would be so different if that were so.

Our lives revolve around a system we all universally share: a system of values. These values are my foundation and have helped shape my character over the years to make me the man I am today.

The opportunities for unethical behavior are endless, so be vigilant, aware when an ethical decision lies before you, an ethical decision that can be answered through professing a set of values that defines you as a person. My overarching values have mirrored the Marine Corps values of Honor, Courage and Commitment. When you tie these values to the values I received from my family and the culture I was born into, it defines me as the person I am today. The tie-ins in this book are all linked to the values I try to live each and every day: all 86,400 seconds of them.

Everyone at some time in their life is faced with a difficult decision. Each of us responds based on the person we have become and our set of values. Our individual character is a sum of our good habits and bad habits, all tied to our values, whether universal or relative. Sometimes we just don't know the right words to say or how to help someone make them feel good about themselves when they are challenged. My hope is that as you read this book of tie-ins you will see how each story is meant to be shared as we – and those we feel genuine concern for – face difficulties throughout life. These tie-ins are all connected to our wonderful character and the values we profess.

The book's appendix is designed to act as a reference for a particular tie-in as it relates to adversity, appreciation, courage, honor, mentoring, etc. Once you look at one of the reference titles, you can scroll down to one of the tie-ins and use it for the circumstance at hand. A number of the tie-ins can be used for different life circumstances.

Jerome A. Waterman summed it up well when he said, "It is that confidence in the leadership of that man or woman who guides, that enables people to forget the perils of the journey and the darkness of the night."

I sincerely hope this book, and these "tie-ins" help you and yours through the perils in life.

God Bless,
Joseph C. Shusko

1

So, You Want to be a Mentor

Let me start off by asking you what the fastest thing is known to man. What would you say? For years I have been asking people this question and you would be amazed at some of the answers; many of them pretty good: speed, a cheetah, a falcon, light, bar flies, etc. Well, I believe the fastest thing known to man is imagination. Think about that for a second.

Imagine there is a bank that credits your account $86,400 every day. It carries no balance and every evening it deletes what you don't use. What would you do with it?

Each of us has that bank account; it's called time. Every morning it credits you with 86,400 seconds and every evening it writes off what you don't use. There are 86,400 seconds in a 24-hour period. After that, it has no balance, we start all over again.

Each day you have a new account. If you fail to use those deposits, you can't go back. Live in the present. Live for today. The clock is running. Life is not a dress rehearsal; you only get one chance at it. Make the very best of everything you have. Take responsibility for your life. Make a difference in your life and the lives of others. Write down at the end of the day how you have made a difference. Don't watch the world go by, act now!

You would surely spend every penny of the $86,400; spend the seconds just as well! ~ Author Unknown

Okay, but I don't have the time to work on my finances; work on my fitness; eat right, etc. I work an eight to ten hour day five days a week.

My answer would be, yes you do have the time. Let me explain.

Life is so precious. You're only on this planet a very short time. Some say you're only on this planet for about 3900 weekends. It really doesn't matter, whether you're on this planet 3900 weekends or 5000 weekends. The bottom-line, life is not a dress rehearsal. You only get one chance to get it right. Don't put off tomorrow what you can do today. Don't have any regrets. Make an effort daily to write down the things you want to do and the things you need to do. Prioritize those events and then make it happen. Anything is possible if you have a plan. The issue at hand is time, you only have so much. Today the time is right to do anything you want, so just do it!

The Time is truly right to do the things you want to do today. Again, there are no guarantees in life. You have to take the full measure of what gifts you have been given. You may say, "I see what you mean, but how do I crunch all the things I have to do in a day with only 86,400 seconds."

I'm glad you asked me that; read on.

A Marine stood before his Marines with a number of items spread in front of him on a table. When he started his class, he picked up a large jar and proceeded to fill it with golf balls. He asked his Marines if the jar was full, and they agreed that it was full. The Marine then picked up a box of marbles and poured them in the jar and again asked his Marines if the jar was full and they agreed. Then he picked up a box of sand and poured it in the jar and asked his Marines if the jar was full and once again they agreed. The Marine then poured two cups of coffee in the jar filling all the empty space to show the Marines the jar still was not full until the liquid was added.

He then told his Marines the jar represents life. The golf balls are the most important things in your life: God, Country, Corps, family and your Marines. The marbles represent other things that matter to you like your house and your car. The sand is everything else or the small stuff in life. If you put the sand in the jar first, there will be no room for the marbles and the golf balls.

The same goes for life. If you spend all your time and energy on the small stuff, you will never have room for the most important things in your life. Pay attention to the things critical to your happiness. Learn to prioritize all your responsibilities. Play with your children. Take time to get medical checkups. Take your partner out to dinner. Play another 18 holes of golf. Take care of the golf balls first.

"What is the coffee for?" asked a young Marine. The Marine answered, "It just goes to show you that no matter how full your life may seem, there is always room to enjoy a cup of coffee with one of your Marines." ~ Author Unknown

Let me explain that very last sentence. Imagine it is closing time at your business on a beautiful Friday afternoon. You look at your watch and it is approaching 5:00 p.m. You're starting to close up shop and one of your employees knocks on your door.

You motion for the person to come on in. You ask him what you can do for him. You're hoping he doesn't have a lot to talk about since your spouse reminded you that dinner will be at 6:00 p.m. and you need to be home early to entertain your guests.

Your employee starts by asking you why they removed Pluto from the solar system. You're thinking, oh my goodness, is he for real? As a leader and as a mentor you only have two options. First, you can ask the employee if he can wait until Monday to discuss his dilemma. If you choose this approach, you have no idea what he may do over the weekend but you can be assured that he will stop believing in you because you did not show genuine concern for his issue. You may lose all ability to lead him.

Your second choice may go something like this: You ask the employee to come in, have a seat and then you ask him, "what can I do for you?" Your employee asks you why they removed Pluto from the solar system. You don't know the answer but you take the phone off the hook, turn the computer off and start peeling the grape on an important issue to one of your employees. You show genuine concern. You may not have the 100% solution regarding his issue but you "shared a cup of coffee" with him and he walks out the door around 6:00 p.m. happy as can be. Your Jar of Life is now truly full with your employee. I can almost promise that individual will be a more productive employee because he saw you genuinely cared for him. When you get home your spouse is going to be pretty upset with you, but that is a different matter for discussion.

The bottom-line is that there is always time to accomplish the things you want to do; you just have to commit yourself to accomplishing them. Also, when dealing with human beings a much smarter man once told me, "without genuine concern you will fail!"

So what is commitment? I'm glad you asked. This is a true story that I heard first hand while visiting Australia years ago. There once was an endurance race in Australia that ran for 544 miles between Melbourne and Sidney. It took most competitors about five days to complete.

One year, a 61-year-old Australian cattleman/potato farmer named Cliff Young showed up to run wearing boots, blue jeans and a flannel shirt. Runners with "go faster" shoes, vented shirts and high speed shorts tried to convince him he was at the wrong place. Others told him he was crazy and that there was no way he could finish the race. He responded by saying, "Yes I can. See, I grew up on a farm where we couldn't afford horses or tractors, and the whole time I was growing up, whenever the storms would roll in, I'd have to go out and round up the sheep. We had 2,000 sheep on 2,000 acres. Sometimes I would have to run those sheep for two or three days. It took a long time, but I'd always catch them. I believe I can run this race."

When the race started, the pros quickly left Cliff behind. The crowds and television audience were entertained because Cliff didn't even run properly, he appeared to shuffle. Many even feared for the old farmer's safety.

When the morning of the second day came, everyone was in for a big surprise. Not only was Cliff still in the race, he had continued jogging all night.

You see, the elite runners forgot to tell the farmer the way they run the race. In order to compete, one had to run about 18 hours a day and sleep the remaining six hours. Cliff Young did not know this unwritten rule.

Eventually Cliff was asked about his tactics for the rest of the race. To everyone's disbelief, he claimed he would run straight through to the finish without sleeping. When tired, he would just lie next to the road for a few hours of sleep.

By the final night, he had surpassed all of the elite runners. He was the first competitor to cross the finish line and he also set a new course record.

The race record has been broken a number of times since using Cliff's strategy. The commitment of this one dedicate, determined cattleman has inspired millions of runners – elite and otherwise. ~ Cliff Young, a National hero in Australia.

The worth of our lives comes not in what we do or whom we know, but by WHO WE ARE. ~ Author Unknown

The stories you just read are what I like to call tie-ins. As described in the introduction, sometimes we just don't know the right word or words to say or how to help someone make them feel good about themselves when they are challenged. These stories help us "mentor" ourselves and others by being able to tackle the many challenges we face on a daily basis. For some reason, people remember short stories. I can go on and on using stories to our everyday challenges.

The tie-ins are all tied to leadership. So, what is leadership? Webster II Dictionary defines it as, "the position or office of a leader. The capacity or ability to lead." The United States Marine Corps defines leadership as the act of influencing others in such a manner as to accomplish a mission. I love the General John Lejeune definition:

"The sum of those qualities of intellect, human understanding and moral character that enables a person to inspire and to control a group of people successfully."

That pretty much sums it up well. The Marine Corps also wraps their definition around 14 well-known character traits as part of their foundation of leadership. They have even given it an acronym so as to remember it better; JJ-DID-TIE-BUCKLE. The Corps also says you don't inherit the ability to lead Marines. You acquire that ability by taking an honest look at yourself stacked up against the following well-known leadership traits:

- Judgment
- Justice
- Dependability
- Initiative
- Decisiveness
- Tact
- Integrity
- Endurance
- Bearing
- Unselfishness
- Courage
- Knowledge
- Loyalty
- Enthusiasm

The Corps goes on further to add 11 principles of leadership. There could even be more and that's okay. One can't be concerned as much about the words as we are about how you apply them in your daily existence. They are simply common sense principles and tied to the leadership traits which make for sound leadership when professed.

- Take responsibility for your actions and the actions of your Marines
- Know yourself and seek self-improvement
- Set the example
- Develop your subordinates
- Insured that a job is understood, then supervise it and carry it through to completion
- Know your Marine and look after their warfare
- Every Marine should be kept informed
- Set goals you can reach
- Make sound and timely decisions
- Know your job
- Teamwork

I'm a little biased when it comes to the above leadership traits and principles because they have been my guiding light for the last 39 years in and around our Corp. They do work when you profess them in everything you do, or don't do.

- The Marine Corps also says leaders influence others toward attaining goals.
- Leaders are proactive.
- Leaders do the right thing.

There are many definitions out there for leadership and most of them are great. The problem is that human beings can come up with great definitions, but then forget them when they are stored on the shelf in a nice bound book. To be a good leader, one must profess those great attributes of leadership on a daily basis.

The best leaders I have come across are those who truly understood that a big part of leadership is mentorship. Today, mentoring is also widely recognized as an extremely beneficial career development tool, regardless of the profession.

Studies have shown that having a mentor is a top factor affecting an employee's success, career satisfaction, their happiness in the workspace, and whether they stay with an organization or not. When people think of mentoring, they often think of an older executive counseling a younger protégé. Or they see a senior officer counseling a junior officer or enlisted person. The senior leader advises the junior employee on all facets of their career, how to navigate the world of work, and what he or she needs to do to get ahead. But mentoring has changed a lot in the last few decades.

The idea that career advice must come from a wise old sage is simply old school. The traditional mentor-protégé relationship is not necessarily a thing of the past, but it's no longer the standard.

Building your career or your life without mentors is like entering a busy four-lane major highway the very first time you strap behind the wheel of a car. Sure, you can attempt it but why would you risk it all? Why not use a mentor to navigate through the challenge?

So, what is a mentor?

Like leadership, there are dozens of definitions out there describing a mentor. The dictionaries would say a mentor is:

- an experienced advisor and supporter;
- a trainer;
- a counselor, tutor, teacher, coach.

Look in the mirror; are you one of these? If so, then you are a mentor to someone.

I have a number of great mentors: Major General Tom Jones . . . my son . . . my daughters . . . my wife . . . my best friends . . . and the list goes on and on. It's almost like I have a mentor for every occasion.

Do you know the origins of the term mentor? Folklore and Greek Mythology defines a mentor as the following: Mentor was the son of Alcimus. In his old age, Mentor was a friend of Odysseus (O-des-c-us) who placed Mentor and Odysseus' foster-brother Eumaeus (E-may-e-us) in charge of his son Telemachus (Tell-lim-ma-cus) and of Odysseus' palace, when Odysseus left for the Trojan War.

Because of Mentor's relationship with Telemachus (Tell-lim-ma-cus), and the disguised Athena's encouragement and practical plans for dealing with personal dilemmas, the personal name Mentor has been adopted in English as a term meaning someone who imparts wisdom to and shares knowledge with a less experienced colleague.

The origins of the mentoring movement in the United States is often traced back to 1904 to a former soldier; Ernest Kent Coulter. He was formerly a journalist and a former Lieutenant Colonel in the United States Army. He took a job at New York City's first juvenile court, and was distressed to observe the harsh fate of children in the court system. Recounting one child's story to a group of businessmen and professionals at a 1904 meeting of the Men's Club of New York City's Central Presbyterian Church, he said: "There is only one possible way to save that youngster: to have some earnest, true man volunteer to be his big brother, to look after him, help him to do right, make the little chap feel that there is at least one human being in this great city, who cares whether he lives or dies." Coulter recruited 39 volunteers at that meeting, and the Big Brothers, Big Sisters mentoring program was born. Over the years, it grew to 500 chapters nationwide, and became the largest and best known mentoring program in the country.

Life is truly about relationships and if you can wrap yourself around great people than you too can truly be great. But it does take work! To be a great mentor you have to be there for your protégé 24/7/365, which translates to 100% of the time. Lastly, you will fail if you don't show Genuine Concern for that protégé. The key to success revolves around Genuine Concern!

So, let's talk about a protégé. Who are these people? The dictionaries would say they are:
- someone who is mentored, a student;
- a pupil, an apprentice;
- a person whose welfare, training, or career is advanced by an influential person.

I have a favorite tie-in that summarizes what a protégée is; it's called the Wooden Bowl.

A frail old man went to live with his son, daughter-in-law and 4-year-old grandson. The old man's hands trembled, his eyesight was blurred and his step faltered. The family ate together at the table, but the elderly grandfather's shaky hands and failing sight made eating difficult. Peas rolled off his spoon onto the floor. When he grasped the glass, milk spilled on the tablecloth. The son and daughter-in-law became irritated with the mess. "We must do something about father," said the son. "I've had enough of his spilled milk, noisy eating and food on the floor."

So the husband and wife set a small table in the corner. There, grandfather ate alone while the rest of the family enjoyed dinner. Since grandfather had broken a dish or two, his food was served in a wooden bowl. When the family glanced in Grandfather's direction, sometimes he had a tear in his eye as he sat alone. Still, the only words the couple had for him were sharp admonitions when he dropped a fork or spilled food. The 4-year-old watched in silence.

One evening before supper, the father noticed his son playing with wood scraps on the floor. He asked the child, "What are you making?" The boy responded, "Oh, I am making a little bowl for you and mom to eat your food in when I grow up." The 4-year-old smiled and went back to work. The words struck the parents so that they were speechless, then tears started to stream down their cheeks. Though no word was spoken, both knew what must be done.

That evening the husband took the grandfather's hand and gently led him back to the family table. And for some reason, neither the husband nor wife seemed to care any longer when a fork was dropped, milk spilled or the tablecloth soiled. ~ Author Unknown

Why do I like this tie-in as a great story about a protégé? Each and every one of us is a mentor of some sort. In that capacity there are many protégés constantly watching our every move and looking at the things we do or don't do. Our protégés are constantly taking away experiences that will form their character: both good and bad. You are a direct reflection of your actions, so act ethically in everything you do.

Next, I will break mentorship down a little and show you how to be a successful mentor.

We now know what a mentor and a protégé is. Is there a set of rules for mentors? Standard Operating Procedures? I don't think so. All you need are a few general guiding principles that I have been collecting over the years from others that seem to work:

1. Mentoring can be both <u>a professional and/or personal</u> relationship between two people. That relationship can be <u>formal or informal</u>. Having something in common between both people can help, but it is not absolutely necessary. The biggest requirement is the <u>willingness of both people</u> to commit to the relationship and to follow the principles of mentorship. This willingness also requires truly understanding what mentorship is.

2. A mentor should play the <u>role of advisor, coach, tutor, sponsor, counselor, guide, teacher, trainer, role model, father or mother figure.</u> A mentor has to have the desire and time to want to make a difference in a protégé.

3. A mentee/protégé should be <u>honest, prepared, professional, accepting, compliant, willing, proactive and respectful.</u> A mentee must be willing to learn from his or her mentor.

4. During the first meeting, both the mentor and mentee must be able to <u>adequately express themselves in a two-way process</u> where both parties are <u>free to speak without any barriers.</u> Having some sort of ice-breaker helps. They must accept constructive feedback.

5. Performing <u>an honest assessment of yourself is essential for success.</u> In the Marine Corps we actually have a form that allows the mentee to answer a number of non-threatening questions about themselves. The questionnaire is tied to our Core Values of Honor, Courage and Commitment. This self-assessment document acts as an ice-breaker for both parties. It is an informal assessment/contract between the mentor and mentee, no one else.

6. The mentor has to encourage the mentee to develop a <u>life plan, a dream, and/or an objective with goals</u> to follow; a simple plan where the mentor can help follow and advise the mentee to be successful. Tied

to those goals are the action steps required to achieve the goal. Without them, you will fail.

7. You must use concepts like TLS, taught to me by Major General Jones: *Teach, Learn* and *Smile*. *Teaching* and *learning* can go both ways along the path. When you stop teaching and learning from life experiences you start putting the nails into your coffin. **Smiling** enforces that "universal" language that is appreciated and recognized throughout the world. It's amazing how great things occur when you have that positive attitude topped off with a smile. You are a direct reflection of those around you based on a simple smile.

8. You must have patience. Trust doesn't happen overnight.

9. Be there 24 hours a day, 7 days a week, and 365 days a year . . . unconditionally! This is one of the most important principles of mentoring; being there at any time for any situation. You may not have the exact answer to the challenge, but you're there for the mentee/protégé.

So let me tie this concept of mentorship in with another of my favorite tie-ins. I call this the mentoring quiz. Please take it and see how you do. You'll be surprised to see you truly are a mentor to many.

Name five of the wealthiest people on earth, without looking it up.

1.
2.
3.
4.
5.

Name the last five Heisman Trophy recipients. Can you do it from memory?

1.
2.
3.
4.
5.

Name the last five Miss America pageant winners.

1.
2.
3.
4.
5.

Name the last five winners of the Nobel Peace Prize.

1.
2.
3.
4.
5.

Name the last five Academy Award winners for best actress.

1.

2.

3.

4.

5.

Name five of the last decade's World Series winners along with the year.

1.

2.

3.

4.

5.

The list of questions can go on and on.

None of us always remember yesterday's headlines. There are no second rate achievers in the answers above. They are the best in their fields, but applause dies. Awards tarnish. Achievements are forgotten. Certificates are buried with their owners.

Now please do the following:

Name a few teachers who aided your journey through school.

1.

2.

3.

4.

Name three friends who have helped you through difficult times.

1.
2.
3.

Name five people who have taught you something worthwhile.

1.
2.
3.
4.
5.

Think of a few people who have made you feel appreciated and special.

1.
2.
3.
4.
5.

Think of five people with whom you enjoy spending time.

1.
2.
3.
4.
5.

Name five heroes whose stories have inspired you.

1.
2.
3.
4.
5.

How did you do?

The people who make a difference in your life are not the ones with the most credentials, the most money or the most awards; they are the ones who care. They have "genuine concern" for your welfare. They are your mentors, coaches, teachers, fathers and mothers. ~ Author Unknown

Take the challenge and go out and make a difference in the lives of your family, your friends, and your co-workers by being a mentor. It's a better life when you give of yourself to others.

The last thing I'd like to leave you with is a little "ditty" one of my mentors, Major General Jones taught me a long time ago. I've changed it a bit to reflect my life style but it works no matter how you use it. It's called the 5-4-3-2-1. I definitely can't do this concept the justification like Major General Jones does but I work at it on a daily basis. Let me explain:

Can you tell me what the **five** most important words are when put together to act as a phrase? Think about it.

. . ."**All men are created equal**"

Do you know where that came from?

Most people credit that phrase to Thomas Jefferson. The quote "All men are created equal" has been called an "immortal declaration" and "perhaps" the single phrase of the United States Revolutionary period with the most grand "continuing importance". Thomas Jefferson first used the phrase in the Declaration of Independence as a rebuttal to the popular political theory of the day: the Divine Right of Kings. It was thereafter quoted or incorporated into speeches by a wide array of substantial figures in American political and social life in the United States, and by Dr. Martin Luther King, President Ronald Reagan and a host of others. It has been said that the final form of the phrase was stylized by Benjamin Franklin.

I read that the great doctrine "All men are created equal" incorporated into the Declaration of Independence by Thomas Jefferson, was paraphrased from the writings of Philip Mazzei, an Italian-born patriot and pamphleteer, who was Jefferson's close friend. A few alleged scholars tried to discredit Mazzei as the creator of this statement and the idea by saying that "there is no mention of it anywhere until after the Declaration was published". But this wonderful phrase appears in Mazzei's own hand, written in Italian, several years prior to the writing of the Declaration of Independence.

Phillip Mazzei and Thomas Jefferson both lived in Virginia and often exchanged ideas about true liberty and freedom. No one man can take complete credit for the ideals of American democracy. Mazzei was an Italian physician and a promoter of liberty. He was a close friend of Thomas Jefferson and acted as an agent to purchase arms for Virginia during the American Revolutionary War.

I love sharing the following story about that wonderful phrase. Quite a few years ago I was invited to attend a Freedom Alliance seminar hosted by Lieutenant Colonel Oliver "Ollie" North in Philadelphia, Pennsylvania. After the wonderful speeches, we all sat for dinner and I noticed a single empty chair at our table. A moment or two later, Thomas Jefferson and Quincy Adams walked into the room dressed in the period of their lives.

Thomas Jefferson came to our table and sat with us as we ate our dinner. He was great and spoke as if we were living in his era. When he finished talking to us he asked if anyone had any questions. I couldn't miss the opportunity so I asked him, "Mr. President, did you actually coin the phrase 'All men are created equal?'" He hesitated for a moment and I thought to myself, I got him. Then without missing a beat he started discussing how his Italian patriot friend Phillip Mazzei gave that phrase to him when he was struggling with the exact words to write in the Declaration of Independence. I was impressed. As the evening was ending, I went up to this young man impersonating Thomas Jefferson and told him I was impressed he knew that often overlooked story.

But does it really matter who coined that beautiful phrase? It's just a shame we have such a beautiful phrase but it is seldom practiced. Imagine if we all practiced those wonderful words on a daily basis. What a life we would have. What a beautiful world we would live in. I'll go one further and say, "God created all men and women equal."

What are the **four** most favorite words in the English language that when put together also make a phrase? **Live a balanced life.**

Can you tell me what an equal lateral triangle is, Major General Jones would ask? It's a three side object where all three sides are equal. Label the left side with M, for mental. Label the right side with P, for physical. Label the bottom side with S, for spiritual. Label the inside of the triangle with E, for emotional. The acronym to remember this by is MEPS: mental, emotional, physical and spiritual.

Strive to live your life in a balanced way where you spend equal time in each of the sides of the triangle.

The M is for mental. It's about your dreams and goals in life. What do you want to do with your life? In my leadership style, all Marines who work for me are required to write down three personal and professional goals. We review the goals together whenever possible. I remind them to work diligently to achieve their goals and if I can help along that path, I'm there for them. It's incredibly rewarding and puts a smile on my face when they achieve their goals and thank me for the guidance.

The P is for physical. It's not just about what type of physical condition you're in, although staying in shape does help live a balance life. What I'm talking about are the action steps you'll need to create to be successful at achieving your dreams and goals. It would be extremely difficult to achieve your goals if you don't write down all the action steps it will take you to attain those goals. Sometimes this is the most difficult part of the MEPS triangle. It's pretty easy to come up with a goal. The challenge comes when you actually have to sit down and build the "action steps" to achieve that goal. I love seeing people set and achieve goals because they had a plan. This is the physical part of MEPS.

The S is for spiritual. Have a solid, sound base for everything you do; a strong foundation. Building your goals in sand will cause them to shift and eventually fail. You need to have a solid foundation of values. You learn values from your family, your schools, your church and your friends. Build that foundation to hold the weight of the world on your shoulders.

The E is for emotional. These are your connecting files with self and others. This is especially pertinent if you have people who work for you or if you have children; family. How are you going to connect with them regarding the mental, physical and spiritual parts of your life?

The bottom-line is: if you only spend time on one side of the triangle you'll eventually lead a flat line which in medical jargons would be fatal. Strive to live a balance life in everything you do.

What are the three most favorite words in the English language that when put together make a phrase? **I love you.** It's not too tough to tell others you love them as people. The following tie-in called Unconditional Love explains it best.

This is a tie-in about a soldier who was coming home after Vietnam. He called his parents from San Francisco.

"Mom, Dad, I'm coming home but I have a favor to ask of you. I want to bring home a friend." "Sure," they replied, "we'd love to meet him."

"There is something you should know," the son said, "He was hurt pretty bad in the war. He stepped on a mine and lost an arm and leg. He has nowhere to go. I'd like him to live with us."

"I'm sorry to hear that son, maybe we can find a place for him to live." They said.

"No mom and dad, I want him to live with us."

"Son, you don't know what you're asking. Someone with such a handicap will be a troubling burden on us all. We'll need to build ramps and make other modifications to the house. We have our own lives to live and we can't let something like this interfere. I think you should just come home now and not worry so much about this guy; he'll find a way to live on his own."

At that point, the son hung up the phone. The parents heard nothing from him for days. About a week went by when they got a call from the San Francisco Police Department. The officer said a young man died after falling from a building and they thought it was their son. He said, it looked like it could be suicide.

The grief-stricken parents flew out to San Francisco and were taken to the morgue to identify the body. When the coroner pulled out the body, sure enough, it was their son. They recognized him but to their horror they discovered he only had one arm and one leg.

It's easy to love those who are good-looking or fun to be around, but we don't like people who inconvenience us or make us uncomfortable. Accept people as they are. ~ Author Unknown

It comes back down to "God created all men equal." Treat others like you want to be treated and it's amazing how beautiful life can be.

What are the two most favorite words? **Genuine Concern.**

Simply put, genuine concern is being there for others 24 hours a day, 7 days a week, and 365 days a year, and having that listening skill that is sincere, genuine and appreciated. It's about being real and not pretentious. If you are genuine then others will approve of you because of your honestly, truthfulness, your uprightness and Integrity in dealing with relationships. Showing soundness of moral principle and character is vital. Without genuine concern, you will fail. You can't fool others when it comes to showing genuine concern.

What is the single most favorite word when it comes to leadership? **Humility.**

A true mentor realizes he or she is not better than their protégée. They have respect for others, all others. Being grounded as a good person is imperative. Humility enhances leadership effectiveness in mentoring others if done properly. It's about understanding your limitations, capabilities, your openness and awareness of others.

Okay, I think you get it now. I've attempted to tell my story by using tie-ins. Stories are so powerful when dealing with challenges in life and when you can't find the exact phrase, sentence or word to work through the issues.

You can use stories for just about every situation you are up against. The key is to have genuine concern and passion when applying these stories. Each and every one of these stories has touched my life in some magically way. These tie-ins help me remain grounded in everything I do. I'm not perfect but when I tell myself or others a story, it's not only helping the other person, it's recalibrating my moral compass.

Allow these stories to encourage you to know you are truly a special person, a father figure, a mother figure, a sister and/or brother, a friend, a mentor and only you can fulfill the purpose to which you were put on this earth to achieve. Understand that you can truly make a difference in your life and the lives of others. As Winston Churchill once said, "Never, never, never quit!"

2

Glass of Milk

One day a poor boy who was selling goods door to door to pay his way through school, found he had only one thin dime left and he was hungry. He decided he would ask for a meal at the next house. However, he lost his nerve when a lovely woman opened the door. Instead of a meal he asked for a drink of water. She thought he looked hungry so she brought him a large glass of milk. He drank it slowly and asked "how much do I owe you?" "You don't owe me anything," said the woman. "Mother has taught us never to accept pay for kindness." "Then I thank you from the bottom of my heart," said the boy. As Howard Kelly left that house he not only felt physically stronger but his faith in God was also stronger. He had been ready to give up and quit.

Many years later that same young woman became critically ill. The local doctors were baffled. They finally sent her to the big city to specialists for rare diseases. Dr. Kelly was called in for the consultation. When he heard the name of the town she came from, a strange light filled his eyes. Immediately, he rose and went down the hall to the room and he recognized her at once. He went back to the consultation room and was determined to save her life. After a long struggle the battle was won.

Dr. Kelly immediately requested the business office to pass the final bill to him for approval. He looked at it, wrote something on the edge, and the bill was sent to her room. She feared to open it, for she was sure it would take the rest of her life to pay for it all. Finally she looked, and something caught her attention on the side of the bill, it read, "Paid in full with one glass of milk," signed Doc Kelly. Tears of joy flooded her eyes as her happy heart prayed: "Thank you God. Your love has spread broad through human hearts and hands."

The good deed you do today may benefit you or someone you love at the least expected time. If you never see the deed again at least you will have made the world a better place. Isn't that what life is about? ~ Author Unknown

President Eisenhower used to demonstrate the art of leadership with a simple piece of string. He'd put it on the table and say, "pull it, and it will follow anywhere you wish. Push it, and it will go nowhere at all."

3

The Brick

About ten years ago, a young and very successful executive named Josh was traveling down a Chicago neighborhood street. He was going a bit fast in his new 12-cylinder Jaguar XKE, which was only two months old.

He was watching for kids darting out from between parked cars and slowed down when he thought he saw something. As his car passed, no children appeared. Instead, a brick smashed into the Jag's side door! He slammed on the brakes and backed the Jag back to the spot where the brick had been thrown. Josh jumped out of the car, grabbed the nearest kid and pushed him up against a parked car shouting, "What was that all about and who are you? Just what the heck are you doing? That's a new car and that brick you threw is going to cost you a lot of money. Why did you do it?"

The young boy was apologetic. "Please, mister...please, I'm sorry but I didn't know what else to do," he pleaded. "I threw the brick because no one else would stop." With tears dripping down his face and off his chin, the youth pointed to a spot just around a parked car. "It's my brother, mister," he said. "He rolled off the curb and fell out of his wheelchair and I can't lift him up." Now sobbing, the boy asked the stunned executive, "Will you please help me get him back into his wheelchair? He's hurt and he's too heavy for me."

Moved beyond words, the driver tried to swallow the rapidly swelling lump in his throat. Straining, he lifted the handicapped boy back into the wheelchair, then took out a linen handkerchief and dabbed at the fresh scrapes and cuts. A quick look told him everything was going to be okay. "Thank you and may God bless you," the grateful child told the stranger. Too shook up for words, the man simply watched the boy push his wheelchair-bound brother down the sidewalk toward their home.

It was a long, slow walk back to the Jaguar. The damage was very noticeable. Josh never bothered to repair the dented side door. He kept the dent there to remind him of this message: "Don't go through life so fast that someone has to throw a brick at you to get your attention!"

God whispers in our souls and speaks to our hearts. Sometimes when we don't have time to listen, He has to throw a brick at us. It's our choice to listen or not. ~ Author Unknown

The best index to a person's character is (a) how he treats people who can't do him any good, and (b) how he treats people who can't fight back. ~ A. Van Buren

4

Obstacles in Our Path

In ancient times, a king had a boulder placed on a roadway. Then he hid himself and watched to see if anyone would remove the huge rock. Some of the king's wealthiest merchants and courtiers came by and simply walked around it. Others loudly blamed the king for not keeping the roads clear, but none did anything about getting the stone out of the way. Then a peasant came along carrying a load of vegetables. Upon approaching the boulder, the peasant laid down his burden and tried to move the stone to the side of the road. After much pushing and straining, he finally succeeded. After the peasant picked up his load of vegetables, he noticed a purse lying in the road where the boulder had been. The purse contained many gold coins and a note from the king indicating that the gold was for the person who removed the boulder from the roadway. The peasant learned what many of us never understand: every obstacle presents an opportunity to improve our condition. ~ Author Unknown

5

Pickup in the Rain

One night, around 11:30 p.m., an older African-American woman was standing on the side of an Alabama highway trying to endure a lashing rain storm. Her car had broken down and she desperately needed a ride.

Soaking wet, she decided to flag down the next car. A young white man stopped to help her, generally unheard of in those conflict-filled 1960's. The man took her to safety, helped her get assistance and put her into a taxicab. She seemed to be in a big hurry, but wrote down his address and thanked him.

Seven days went by and a knock came on the man's door. To his surprise, a giant console color TV was delivered to his home. A special note was attached. It read: "Thank you so much for assisting me on the highway the other night. The rain drenched not only my clothes, but also my spirits. Then you came along. Because of you, I was able to make it to my dying husband's bedside just before he passed away. God bless you for helping me and unselfishly serving others." ~ Author Unknown

Judge a man's character not by what he drives, but what drives him and how he treats all mankind. ~ Author Unknown

6

Keep Your Fork

There was a young woman who had been diagnosed with a terminal illness and had been given three months to live. As she was getting her things in order, she contacted her pastor and had him come to her house to discuss her final wishes. She told him which songs she wanted sung at the service, what scriptures she would like read and what outfit she wanted to be buried in.

Everything was in order and the pastor was preparing to leave when the young woman suddenly remembered something very important to her. "There's one more thing," she said excitedly. "What's that?" the pastor's reply. "This is very important; I want to be buried with a fork in my right hand." The pastor stood looking at the young woman, not knowing quite what to say. "That surprises you, doesn't it?" the young woman asked. "Well, to be honest, I'm puzzled," said the pastor. The young woman explained.

"My grandmother once told me this story. I have also always tried to pass along its message to those I love and those who are in need. In all my years of attending church socials and potluck dinners, I always remember when the dishes of the main course were being cleared; someone would inevitably lean over and say, 'Keep your fork.' It was my favorite part because I knew something better was coming – like chocolate cake or apple pie. Something wonderful, and with substance! So, I just want people to see me there in that casket with a fork in my hand and I want them to wonder, what's with the fork? Tell them to keep your fork – the best is yet to come."

The pastor's eyes welled up with tears of joy as he hugged the young woman good-bye. He knew this would be one of the last times he would see her before her death. But he also knew that the young woman had a better grasp of heaven than he did. She had a better grasp of what heaven would be like than many people twice her age, with twice as much experience and more knowledge. She KNEW that something better was coming.

So the next time you reach down for your fork, let it remind you ever so gently that the best is yet to come.

Friends are a very rare jewel. They make you smile and encourage you to succeed. They lend an ear, they share a word of praise, and they always want to open their hearts to us. Show your friends how much you care. Remember to always be there for them, even when you need them more. Cherish the time you have and the memories you share. ~ Author Unknown

The one who has faith, no explanation is necessary. To one without faith, no explanation is possible. ~ Saint Thomas Aquinas

Humility must always be the portion of any man who receives acclaim even in the blast of his followers and the sacrifices of his friends. ~ Dwight Eisenhower

7

The Jar of Life

Marine stood before his Marines with items in front of him. When he started his class, he picked up a large jar and proceeded to fill it with golf balls. He asked his Marines if the jar was full, and they agreed. The Marine then picked up a box of marbles and poured them in the jar and again asked his Marines if the jar was full and they agreed. He then picked up a box of sand and poured it in the jar and asked his Marines if the jar was full and once again they agreed. The Marine then poured two cups of coffee in the jar filling all the empty space to show the Marines the jar still wasn't full until the liquid was added. Then he told his Marines the jar represents life. The golf balls are the most important things in your life ~ your God, Country, Corps, family and your Marines. The marbles represent the things that matter to you like your house, your dog, and your car, etc. The sand is everything else or the small stuff in life. If you put the sand in the jar first, there will be no room for the marbles and the golf balls.

The same goes for life. If you spend all your time and energy on the small stuff, you will never have room for the things most important in your life. Pay attention to the things critical to your happiness. Learn to prioritize all your responsibilities. Play with your children. Take time to get medical checkups. Take your partner out to dinner. Play another 18 holes of golf. Take care of the golf balls first. "What is the coffee for," asked a young devil dog. The Marine said, "It just goes to show you that no matter how full your life may seem, there is always room to enjoy a cup of coffee with one of your Marines." ~ Author Unknown

Every time you smile at someone, it is an action of love, a gift to that person, a beautiful thing. ~ Mother Teresa

8

Puppies for Sale

A farmer had some puppies he needed to sell. He painted a sign advertising the pups and set about nailing it to a post. As he was putting the last nail in he felt a tug on his overalls. He looked down to see a young boy. "Mister," he said, "I want to buy one of your puppies." "Well" said the farmer, "these puppies come from fine parents and cost a lot of money."

The boy dropped his head for a moment reached into his pockets and pulled out a handful of change to hold up for the farmer. "I've got 39 cents, is that enough?" "Sure" said the farmer. And with that he called his dog, Dolly. Out of the doghouse ran Dolly with four little balls of fur following. The little boy pressed his face against the fence his eyes dancing with delight. As the dog came to the fence he noticed something else stirring inside the doghouse. Slowly another puppy appeared sliding down the ramp. Then in an awkward manner the little fur ball began hobbling towards the others. "I want that one," said the boy. The farmer knelt down and said, "Son, you don't want that puppy. He will never be able to run and play like the others." With that the little boy stepped back from the fence, reached down and rolled up one leg of his trousers. In doing so, he revealed a steel brace running down both sides of his leg attached to a special shoe. Looking back at the farmer he said, "You see sir, I don't run too well myself and he will need someone who understands." ~ Author Unknown

The world is full of people who need someone who understands. ~ Author Unknown

9

The Echo of Life

A son and his father were walking in the mountains. Suddenly the son falls, hurts himself and screams: "AAAhhhh!"

To his surprise, he hears the voice repeating somewhere in the mountains: "AAAhhhh!"

Curious, he yells: "Who are you?" He receives the answer: "Who are you?"

And then he screams: "I hate you!" and the voice answers: "I hate you!"

Angered by the response he yells: "coward" and he receives the answer: "coward!"

He looks to his father and asks: "What's going on?" The father smiles and says: "Son, pay attention."

The man screams: "You're a champion!" The voice answers: "You're a champion!"

The boy is surprised but doesn't understand.

Then the father explains: "People call this an echo, but really this is life. It gives you back everything you say or do. Our life is simply a reflection of our actions. If you want more love in the world, create more love in your heart. If you want more competence in your team, improve your competence. This relationship applies to everything, in all aspects of life; Life will give you back everything you have given to it." ~ Author Unknown

Your life is not a coincidence; it's a reflection of you! ~ Author Unknown

A good leader inspires confidence in himself, a great leader inspires followers' confidence in themselves. ~ Author Unknown

A leader leads by example, whether he intends to or not. ~ Author Unknown

10

The Wooden Bowl

A frail old man went to live with his son, daughter-in-law, and 4-year-old grandson. The old man's hands trembled, his eyesight was blurred, and his step faltered. The family ate together at the table, but the elderly grandfather's shaky hands and failing sight made eating difficult. Peas rolled off his spoon onto the floor. When he grasped the glass, milk spilled on the tablecloth. The son and daughter-in-law became irritated with the mess. "We must do something about father," said the son. "I've had enough of his spilled milk, noisy eating and food on the floor."

So the husband and wife set a small table in the corner. There, grandfather ate alone while the rest of the family enjoyed dinner. Since grandfather had broken a dish or two, his food was served in a wooden bowl! When the family glanced in Grandfather's direction, sometimes he had a tear in his eye as he sat alone. Still, the only words the couple had for him were sharp admonitions when he dropped a fork or spilled food. The 4-year-old watched in silence.

One evening before supper, the father noticed his son playing with wood scraps on the floor; He asked the child, "What are you making?" The boy responded, "Oh, I am making a little bowl for you and mom to eat your food in when I grow up." The four year old smiled and went back to work. The words struck the parents so that they were speechless, then tears started to stream down their cheeks. Though no word was spoken, both knew what must be done.

That evening the husband took the grandfather's hand and gently led him back to the family table. And for some reason, neither the husband nor wife seemed to care any longer when a fork was dropped, milk spilled or the tablecloth soiled.

I've learned that, no matter what happens, how bad it seems today, life does go on, and it will be better tomorrow.

I've learned that you can tell a lot about a person's character by the way he or she handles themselves with the following four things:

1. A rainy day,
2. The elderly,
3. Lost luggage, and
4. Tangled Christmas tree lights.

Regardless of your relationship with your parents, you will miss them when they are gone. Life sometimes gives you a second chance. Don't go through life with a catcher's mitt on both hands. You need to be able to throw something back. You need to focus on your family and friends and do the best you can. ~ Author Unknown

Let us always meet each other with a smile, for the smile is the beginning of love. ~ Mother Teresa

11

A Dad's Blessings

A young man was getting ready to graduate from college. For many months he had admired a sports car in a dealer's showroom and knowing his dad could well afford it, he told him that the car was all he wanted.

As graduation day approached, the young man awaited signs that his dad had purchased the car. Finally, on the morning of his graduation, his dad called him into his private study. His dad told him how proud he was to have such a fine son, and told him how much he loved him. He handed his son a beautifully wrapped gift box. Curious, but somewhat disappointed, the young man opened the box and found a lovely, leather bound Bible, with the young man's name embossed in gold. Angry, he raised his voice to his dad and said "with all your money, you give me a Bible?" and stormed from the house leaving the Bible.

Many years passed and the young man was very successful in business. He had a beautiful home and a wonderful family, but realized his dad was very old, and thought perhaps he should go to him. He had not seen him since that graduation day. Before he could make arrangements, he received a telegram telling him his dad had passed away, and willed all of his possessions to his son. He needed to come home immediately and take care of things.

When he arrived at his dad's house, sudden sadness and regret filled his heart. He began to search through his dad's important papers and saw the still new Bible, just as he had left it years ago. With a tear in his eyes, he opened the Bible and began to turn the pages. As he did, a car key dropped from the back of the Bible. It had tag with the dealer's name, the same dealer who had the sports car he had desired. On the tag was the date of his graduation, and the words PAID IN FULL. ~ Author Unknown

How many times do we miss the Spirit's blessings and answers to our prayers because they don't arrive exactly as we have expected.

12

Building Your House

An elderly carpenter was ready to retire. He told his boss of his plans to leave the house-building business to live a more leisurely life with his wife and enjoy his extended family. He would miss the money each week, but he wanted to retire. The boss was sorry to see his good worker go and asked if he could build one more house as a personal favor. The carpenter said yes, but over time it was easy to see that his heart was not in his work. He resorted to shoddy workmanship and used inferior materials. It was an unfortunate way to end a dedicated career.

When the carpenter finished his work his boss came to inspect the home. Then he handed the keys for the front door to the carpenter and said, this is your house, my gift to you. The carpenter was shocked. What a shame. If he had only known he was building his own house, he would have done it so differently.

Many of us often follow a path similar to that of the carpenter's. We build our lives, a day at a time, often putting less than our best into the building. Then, with a shock, we realize we have to live in the house we built. If we could do it over, we would do it much differently, but you can't go back. You are the carpenter, and every day you hammer a nail, place a board, or erect a wall, you're building the house you will live in. Life is a do-it-yourself project. Your attitude and the choices you make today help

build the house you will live in tomorrow. Build wisely!
~ Author Unknown

A truly happy person is one who can enjoy the scenery of a detour. ~ Author Unknown

13

Pity Party and the Mindset to Live

There once was a registered nurse, who was also a Marine reservist. He was activated and deployed to Iraq and while on a patrol, a suicide bomber in a car charged his position. All of his Marines dove for cover while he stood his ground emptying his rifle into the driver until eventually the car stopped. Unfortunately, the vehicle did not stop immediately and exploded launching him backwards against barriers severing both his legs at the thigh.

A corpsman came up and started gathering the wounded. The registered nurse Marine grabbed his severed legs and crawled to the helicopter. There was only so much room on the aircraft and one of the corpsman, noticing the registered nurse Marine had the worse injuries, bumped everyone else off the aircraft and put him on. The helicopter transported him to the battalion aid station where another corpsman was waiting to put a catheter in the registered nurse Marine. The corpsman attempting to put the catheter in the registered nurse Marine was having a difficult time, shaking and throwing up. The registered nurse Marine took the catheter from the young corpsman and set it himself. He had the mindset to survive. ~ Author Unknown

14

The Butterfly

A man found a cocoon with a small opening. He sat and watched a butterfly for several hours as it struggled to force its body through the little hole. Then it seemed to stop making any progress. It appeared to get as far as it could.

The man decided to help by taking a pair of scissors and snipped off the remaining bit of the cocoon. The butterfly emerged easily but was swollen with shriveled wings. The man kept watching expecting the wings to expand to support the body. It never happened. In fact, the butterfly spent the rest of its short life crawling around with a swollen body and shriveled wings. It never flew. What the man, in his kindness and haste, did not understand was that the restricting cocoon and the struggle required for the butterfly to get through the tiny opening was God's way of forcing fluid from the body into its wings so that it would be ready for flight once it freed itself from the cocoon.

Sometimes struggles are exactly what we need in our lives. If God allowed us to go through our lives without obstacles, it would cripple us. We could never be as strong as what we could have been. Struggles in Life are sometimes necessary. ~ Author Unknown

It may be that your sole purpose in life is simply to be kind to others. ~ Author Unknown

15

86,400 Seconds

Imagine there is a bank that credits your account $86,400 every day. It carries no balance and every evening it deletes what you don't use. What would you do with it?

Each of us has that bank account; it's called time. Every morning it credits you with 86,400 seconds and every evening it writes off what you don't use. It has no balance.

Each day you have a new account. If you fail to use those deposits, you can't go back.

Live in the present. Live for today. The clock is running. Make the best of everything you have. Take responsibility for your life. Make a difference. Write down at the end of the day how you've made a difference. Don't watch the world go by.

You would spend every penny of the $86,400; spend the seconds just as well! ~ Author Unknown

The average human heart beats 100,000 times a day, make every beat count. ~ Author Unknown

16

The Window and the Pursuit of Happiness

Two seriously ill men occupied the same hospital room. One man was allowed to sit up in his bed for one hour a day to drain the fluids from his lungs. His bed was next to the only window in the room. The other man had to lie flat all the time. The men talked for hours. They spoke of family and friends. Every evening when the one man was allowed to sit up he would describe what was outside his window. The man in the other bed lived for that one hour period each day. "The window overlooked a park with a lovely lake," the man said. Ducks and swans played. Kids sailed boats. Lovers walked hand in hand. The man would lie there with his eyes closed imagining what the other man was describing.

One day while the man was describing the parade go by, the man confined to lying on his back said to himself, why should he have all the pleasures of seeing everything while I can't. It didn't seem fair. He soon started to be resentful and his manner turned sour. He started to brood and found himself unable to sleep.

Late one night, as he lay looking at the ceiling, the man closest to the window began to cough. He was choking on the fluids in his lungs. The man watched as the man struggled to hit the emergency call button. In less than five minutes the coughing stopped and there was a deathly silence. In the morning the nurse found the man dead. After they removed the dead man from the hospital room the other man asked to be moved to the window bed. Slowly and painfully he propped himself up and looked out the window; a window that faced a brick wall.

The pursuit of happiness is a matter of choice; it is an attitude we choose to express consciously. ~ Author Unknown

Always keep your words soft and sweet, just in case you have to eat them. ~ Author Unknown

17

Emotional Bank Account (EBA)

A 92-year old petite well-poised and proud man dressed himself fully every morning by 8 a.m. He combed his hair fashionably and shaved his face perfectly, even though he was legally blind. One day, he had to move to a nursing home. His wife of 70-years recently passed making the move necessary.

After many hours of waiting patiently in the lobby of the nursing home, he smiled when he was told his room was ready. As he maneuvered his walker to the elevator an orderly wanted to provide the man with a vision of his tiny room. "I love it already!" barked the older gentleman with the enthusiasm of an 8-year old having just been presented a new puppy.

"Mr. Jones, you haven't seen your room yet," said the orderly.

"That doesn't have anything to do with it," the old man replied. "Happiness is something you decide on ahead of time. Whether or not I like my room doesn't depend on how the furniture is arranged, it's how I arrange my mind. I already decided to love it. It's a decision I make every morning when I wake up. I have a choice. I can remain in bed and recount all the difficulties in my life with the parts of my body that no longer work or I can get up and be thankful for what I have. Each day is a gift as long as my eyes are open. I'll focus on the new day and all my happy memories I have stored away. My advice to you is to deposit a lot of happiness in that EBA of memories." ~ Author Unknown

Five Simple rules to live by:
1. Free your heart from hatred.
2. Free your mind from worries.
3. Live simply.
4. Give more.
5. Expect less.

~ Author Unknown

18

Never Quit!

One day a farmer's donkey fell into a well. The animal cried for hours as the farmer tried to figure out what to do. Finally, he decided the animal was really old and the well needed to be covered up anyway. It just wasn't worth it to retrieve the donkey, so he invited his neighbors to come over to help. They all grabbed shovels and began shoveling dirt into the well. At first the donkey realized what was happening and cried horribly. Then to everyone's amazement he quieted down. A few shovels later the farmer looked down and was astonished to see with each shovel of dirt that hit the donkey's back, he would shake it off and take a step up. Pretty soon everyone was amazed as the donkey stepped up and over the edge of the well and trotted off.

Life is going to shovel dirt on you. The trick to getting out of the well is to shake it off and take that step up. Each of our troubles is a stepping stone. We can get out of the deepest wells just by not stopping, never giving up. Shake it off and step up to the plate.

The donkey later came back and bit the farmer. The farmer eventually died in agony from septic shock due to the bite getting infected.

Moral of the story – when you do something wrong, and try to cover your butt, it always comes back to bite you in the ass. ~ Author Unknown

19

Night Watch

A nurse took the tired, anxious Marine to the bedside. "Your son is here," she said to the old man. She had to repeat the words several times before the man opened his eyes. Heavily sedated because of the pain of his heart attack and medication, he dimly saw the young Marine. He reached out his hand and the Marine wrapped his toughened fingers around his, squeezing a message of love and encouragement.

The Marine sat with the old man all night offering him words of love and strength. Occasionally, the nurse suggested to the Marine to rest awhile. He refused. All through the night the Marine would reassure and calm the old man. The dying man said nothing, just held tightly to his son throughout the night.

As dawn approached, the old man died. The Marine released the lifeless hand and went to get the nurse. While the nurse worked on the old man, the Marine waited. The nurse then went to the Marine to offer words of sympathy, but the Marine interrupted her, "who was that man?" he asked. "He was your father," she replied. "No he wasn't," said the Marine. "I never saw him before in my life."

"Then why didn't you say something when I took you to him?" asked the nurse. "I knew right away there had been a mistake, but I also knew the man needed his son and his son wasn't here. When I knew he was too sick to see I wasn't his son, I stayed." ~ Author Unknown

20

Two Frogs

A group of frogs was hoping in the woods one day when two of them fell into a pit. When the other frogs saw how deep the pit was they yelled down to the two frogs that they were as good as dead. The two trapped frogs ignored the comments and tried to jump out. The other frogs kept yelling to them to stop; that they were as good as dead.

One frog took heed, gave up and laid down to die.

The second frog continued to jump as hard as he could. Once again, the crowd of on-looking frogs yelled at him to stop the pain and just die; to give it up because the situation was hopeless. The frog jumped harder and finally leapt out.

"Thanks, guys," said the newly freed frog as he caught his breath. "I never would have escaped that pit without your encouragement."

One of his friends asked, "Did you not hear us?"

"No, I really couldn't hear what you were saying; I'm deaf, but figured you were all encouraging me the entire time."

There are two lessons in this story:

1. There is power of life and death in the tongue. An encouraging word to someone who is down can lift them up.

2. A destructive word to someone who is down can kill them.

Be careful what you say. Speak life to those who cross your path. Beware of the power of words. Sometimes it is hard to understand that an encouraging word can go such a long way. Anyone can speak words that tend to rob another of the spirit to continue in difficult time.

Special is the individual who will take the time to encourage another. ~ Author Unknown

It is a kindly act to assist the fallen. ~ Mother Teresa

21

The Power of Appreciation

A group of women embarked upon a self-improvement project in their Bible study program at church. Each woman was given homework.

One woman, Carol, came home after the Bible study meeting and asked her husband to help her list six things she could do or change to be a better wife. He was startled by the request and immediately thought he could probably easily list six things or sixty. The husband said "let me think about it and I'll get back to you in the morning, if that's okay."

The next morning Carol's husband stopped at a florist on the way to work. He asked them to send six long-stemmed roses with a note that read: "I can't think of six things I would like you to change, I love you just the way you are."

When the husband came home from work he was greeted by a very happy wife.

The next week at the Bible study the wives compared notes. Some said their husbands wanted them to learn how to cook, to clean the house better, to stop kicking while sleeping, etc. When is was Carol's turn to share her list, she told the group what her husband did and after the Bible study all the women wanted to meet him. It was at this point in his life that he realized the Power of Appreciation.

~ Author Unknown

Accept the challenge so you can feel the exhilaration of victory. ~ General George S. Patton

22

Everyone is Entitled to Make a Mistake

A famous military test pilot was returning from an air show when suddenly both of the plane's engines quit and the aircraft flamed out. By the skill of his abilities he successfully landed but the aircraft was badly damaged. He immediately started inspecting the aircraft and realized it had been fueled with gas instead of jet fuel.

Upon returning to the base, he asked to see the mechanic who serviced the aircraft. The young mechanic got wind of what happened and was sick to his stomach for what he had done. As he headed to meet the pilot, his head was racing. He feared ruining his career, going to Fort Leavenworth prison and could just imagine the pilot's anger. When the young mechanic reported to the pilot, much to his surprise the pilot did not tongue thrash the mechanic for his carelessness and he didn't even criticize him. Instead, he put his arms around the mechanic's shoulders and said, "Son, to show you I'm sure that you'll never do this again, I want you to service my P51 Mustang tomorrow; now go back to work." ~ Author Unknown

Some mistakes are too much fun to only make once.
~ Author Unknown

23

Being a Father Figure

The setting is a perimeter defense in Vietnam, 1968. You are a corporal in B Company 1st Battalion 8th Marines. Your leader, the captain, is being called back to the rear to a meeting of sorts.

You watch him board the CH46 helicopter and it departs. The captain is admired and loved by everyone in his company. You're now scared because a man, your father figure, has left you in the dark.

All of a sudden you receive in-coming fires from an artillery barrage. You start to cry. After a while you see the CH46 helicopter in the distance and it lands in the nearby landing zone and off steps a Marine with railroad tracks on his collar. You are no longer afraid, the captain has returned and all will be well.

You, as a leader, have won the hearts and minds of your Marines. Remember the time you were scared as a youngster and your father came in to chase the boogey man away, it's all about mentoring. ~ Author Unknown

You may be the only one person in the world, but you may also be the world to one person. ~ Author Unknown

24

Dignity and Respect

T
om Jones was a WWII Army pilot and a Harvard graduate. While deployed he started writing to a pen pal, Maggie, much like our Marines are doing today while deployed. This went on for years. Tradition back then said once a pilot hit 25 missions he could come home. So Tom and Maggie started writing about their upcoming first meeting in Boston. No pictures had ever been exchanged. Maggie told Tom she would meet him at the station in a long black dress with a white rose on her lapel at 2100.

At 2100, Tom was there decked out in his uniform. The train emptied and no Maggie. Suddenly from a distance Tom saw two figures approaching. The first one was a beautiful blond with a lovely figure. She walked by and just nodded to Tom. Tom was saying to himself, wow, what a knockout. The next young lady had a long black coat with a white rose. She was just an average looking lady with an average build. Tom was thinking, wish it would have been the blond. Tom then straightened himself up and walked up to the young lady and said, "I'd be honored to take you to dinner Miss Maggie." The lady said, "You've passed the test. You treated me with dignity and respect. The lady you are looking for was the blond who was in front of me. She is waiting for you in that bar across the street."

Well, the rest is history. They wed two weeks later and remain happily married to this day. ~ Author Unknown

Never put both feet in your mouth at the same time, because you won't have a leg to stand on. ~ Author Unknown

25

Operating Out of Assumptions and Paradigms

A woman purchased a package of English shortbread cookies while waiting at Heathrow Airport to board a flight. She sat near her terminal and waited to board. A man approached and indicated by a pleasant gesture that he would like to occupy a seat next to her. She nodded with a yes.

After a few minutes the lady decided to eat some of her cookies. She reached down to grab the cookies, opened the package, and noticed the man besides her watching with great interest. She took the first cookie and ate it. The man then reached down, smiled and took a cookie. The lady ate the cookie in stunned silence. After a moment, she reached in for the third cookie. The, the man once again smiled and without a word grabbed the fourth cookie. The lady's indignation rose as back and forth they went in total silence taking cookies until they reached the bottom of the package with one cookie remaining. Without hesitation, the man took the cookie, broke it in half and cheerfully handed the lady one of the pieces. The woman took it with an icy glare.

After finishing, the man stood, bowed and walked away. The woman couldn't believe anyone could be so rude. She got up and made her way back to the gift store and bought a package of antacid. As she opened her purse to get money, she stopped short; there in her bag were her cookies.

What if he sat next to you on the plane after you just witnessed the full story?"

What would you have done? ~ Author Unknown

If you can't be kind, at least have the decency to be vague. ~ Author Unknown

26

A Gentleman vs. Leading with Fury and Force

Once upon a time the sun and wind quarreled about which was the stronger. The wind said, "I'll prove I am. See the old man down there wearing a coat. I bet I can get his coat off quicker than you can." So the sun went behind a cloud and the wind blew until it was almost a tornado, but the harder it blew the tighter the old man clutched his coat against his body. Finally, the wind gave up and calmed down.

Then the sun came out from behind the clouds and smiled kindly on the old man. Slowly, the old man mopped his brow and pulled off his coat.

The sun then told the wind that gentleness and friendliness are always stronger than fury and force.
~ Author Unknown

Humility must always be the portion of any man who receives acclaim even in the blast of his followers and the sacrifices of his friends. ~ Dwight Eisenhower

27

Being Humble and Making the Best of Life

During the dinner hour, two men jumped in a Mercedes Benz sedan and drove down to the ocean. As they sat on the park bench enjoying the cool breeze they noticed a man getting some things from an older car. As they watched, the man began to canvas the area picking up old bottles, paper and other garbage people left in the sand. The way he was dress indicated this was his job; perhaps a second job. They said to each other, "Look at that poor guy, what a waste! Cleaning up the beach is all he can do. Look at us; we're highly educated, successful and smart. We make all this money and drive beautiful cars. We sure are lucky compared to him."

After a few minutes a young girl came up to the man and began to help him. She'd been sitting on a blanket with several others – evidently her family – a short distance away. So, it became evident the family sitting on the blanket was the man's family. One by one they got up and started helping him. Before long, the cleanup was complete.

Then the man and his family began to play in the sand, laugh and have fun together. The initial attitude of the watching men slowly changed from disdain to envy. They realized that while they had been sitting there basking in their own accomplishments, preparing to go to more meetings, here was someone who had integrated part of his work life with his family, and in many ways, seemed happier than they. ~ Author Unknown

When we treat man as he is, we make him worse than he is; when we treat him as if he already were what he potentially could be, we make him what he should be. ~ Johann Wolfgang von Goethe (1749-1832)

28

Don't Ever be too Full of Yourself

Two battleships were out on maneuvers in heavy weather. Shortly after dark, the lookout on one of the ships said, "Light, bearing on the starboard bow." "Is it steady or moving astern," asked the Captain. "Steady, Sir," replied the young man, which basically meant they were on a collision course.

The Captain told the signalman, "Signal that ship to change course 20 degrees." The return signal read, "Advisable for you to change course 20 degrees."

The Captain said, "The nerve of that man; send him a new signal that says I am the Captain and he needs to change course 20 degrees." Where upon that message, the reply came, "I'm a seaman second class, and you better change course 20 degrees."

By this time the Captain was furious. He spat out, "send him a message that says I am a Captain of a battleship and to change course 20 degrees, immediately." Back came the flashing light, "I'm manning a lighthouse!"
~ Author Unknown

When everything's coming your way, you're in the wrong lane. ~ Author Unknown

29

Always Be Proactive;
Don't Be Reactive

A nurse once took care of the most miserable, ungrateful man you could imagine. Nothing she did was good enough for him. He never said thank you or anything positive. He found fault with everything she did. He made her miserable. So much so that she would take out her frustrations on her family. Other nurses felt the same way. They secretly hoped for his demise.

The nurses were reacting to the old man's behavior. They empowered his weakness to control them. The nurses had the power to choose what to do and did nothing.

One of them finally realized this and also realized she was choosing to be miserable. She could also choose to be proactive and not to be miserable. From that day forth, no matter how horribly he acted, she was never miserable around the old man again.

Think how you can be proactive with your Marines, family, friends and people you meet. ~ Author Unknown

You and only you are responsible for the weather over your head and the grid square where you rest your feet. Make the best of those opportunities! ~ Joe Shusko

30

Values

Awell-known speaker started off his seminar by holding up a $20 bill in a room of 200 executives. He asked, "Who would like this $20 bill?" Hands started going up.

He then said, "I am going to give this $20 to one of you, but first let me do this." He proceeded to crumple the $20 up and then asked, "Who still wants this?" Hands shot up into the air. "Well," he replied, "What if I do this?" He dropped it on the ground and started to grind it into the floor with his shoes. He then picked it up, now all crumpled and dirty and asked, "Now who wants it?" Hands still went into the air.

"My friends, you have all learned a very valuable lesson. No matter what I did to this money, you still wanted it because it did not decrease in value. It was still worth $20. Many times in our lives, we are dropped, crumpled and ground into the dirt by decisions we make and circumstances that come our way. We may feel as though we are worthless. But no matter what has happened or what will happen, you will never lose your value. Don't ever forget it!"

Remember, the people you meet all have the same values. Treat them like you would want to be treated.
~ Author Unknown

31

Commitment

There once was an endurance race in Australia that ran for 544 miles between Melbourne and Sidney. It took most competitors about five days to complete.

One year, a 61-year-old Australian cattleman/potato farmer named Cliff Young showed up to run wearing boots, blue jeans and a flannel shirt. Runners with "go faster" shoes, vented shirts and high speed shorts tried to convince him he was at the wrong place. Others told him he was crazy and that there was no way he could finish the race. He responded by saying, "Yes I can. See, I grew up on a farm where we couldn't afford horses or tractors, and the whole time I was growing up, whenever the storms would roll in, I'd have to go out and round up the sheep. We had 2,000 sheep on 2,000 acres. Sometimes I would have to run those sheep for two or three days. It took a long time, but I'd always catch them. I believe I can run this race."

When the race started, the pros quickly left Cliff behind. The crowds and television audience were entertained because Cliff didn't even run properly, he appeared to shuffle. Many even feared for the old farmer's safety.

When the morning of the second day came, everyone was in for a big surprise. Not only was Cliff still in the race, he had continued jogging all night.

You see, the elite runners forgot to tell the farmer the way they run the race. In order to compete, one had to run about 18 hours a day and sleep the remaining six hours. Cliff Young did not know this unwritten rule.

Eventually Cliff was asked about his tactics for the rest of the race. To everyone's disbelief, he claimed he would run straight through to the finish without sleeping. When tired, he would just lie next to the road for a few hours of sleep.

By the final night, he had surpassed all of the elite runners. He was the first competitor to cross the finish line and he also set a new course record.

The race record has been broken a number of times since using Cliff's strategy. The commitment of this one dedicate, determined cattleman has inspired millions of runners – elite and otherwise. ~ Cliff Young, a National hero in Australia.

The worth of our lives comes not in what we do or whom we know, but by WHO WE ARE. ~ Author Unknown

32

Giving 100%

Joe DiMaggio once played a ball game with a bleeding ulcer and a pulled hamstring. When was his turn to go up and bat, he belted out a line drive to the first baseman. The first baseman picked up the ball and tagged the base before Joe dropped his bat, but that did not slow Joe down. He sprinted to base with all the energy he could muster. Then he walked back to the dugout and passed out.

When he came to his teammates asked him why he had to push so hard. He said, "This may be the only time these people get to see me play. I want to always give 100% for the fans; this may be the only opportunity they have to watch us play."

He also used to be last to leave the dugout because he was a chain smoker and didn't want his fans to get the same bad habit if they saw him smoking. ~ Author Unknown

Always strive to give 100%, you can't give more. ~ Author Unknown

33

Unconditional Love

This is a tie-in about a soldier who was coming home after Vietnam. He called his parents from San Francisco.

"Mom, Dad, I'm coming home but I have a favor to ask of you. I want to bring home a friend." "Sure," they replied, "we'd love to meet him."

"There is something you should know," the son said, "He was hurt pretty bad in the war. He stepped on a mine and lost an arm and leg. He has nowhere to go. I'd like him to live with us."

"I'm sorry to hear that son, maybe we can find a place for him to live." They said.

"No mom and dad, I want him to live with us."

"Son, you don't know what you're asking. Someone with such a handicap will be a troubling burden on us all. We'll need to build ramps and make other modifications to the house. We have our own lives to live and we can't let something like this interfere. I think you should just come home now and not worry so much about this guy; he'll find a way to live on his own."

At that point, the son hung up the phone. The parents heard nothing from him for days. About a week went by when they got a call from the San Francisco Police Department. The officer said a young man died after falling from a building and they thought it was their son. He said, it looked like it could be suicide.

The grief-stricken parents flew out to San Francisco and were taken to the morgue to identify the body. When the coroner pulled out the body, sure enough, it was their son. They recognized him but to their horror they discovered he only had one arm and one leg.

It's easy to love those who are good-looking or fun to be around, but we don't like people who inconvenience us or make us uncomfortable. Accept people as they are. ~ Author Unknown

The most terrible poverty is loneliness and the feeling of being unloved. ~ Mother Teresa

34

Mentoring Quiz

O thers may sometimes ask your advice on what they should do about a personal challenge or taking a next step in life. In other words, they need help sorting out their options and priorities. When mentoring others, a valuable exercise is to have them take this quiz:

- Name five of the wealthiest people on earth
- Name the last five Heisman Trophy winners
- Name the last five winners of Miss America
- Name 10 people who have won the Nobel Peace Prize
- Name the last six Academy Award winners for best actress
- Name the last decade's worth of World Series winners

How did they do?

None of us remember yesterday's headlines. There are no second rate achievers in the answers above. They are the best in their fields, but applause dies. Awards tarnish. Achievements are forgotten. Certificates are buried with their owners.

Now have them do the following:

- Name a few teachers who aided your journey through school
- Name three friends who have helped you through difficult times
- Name five people who have taught you something worthwhile
- Think of a few people who have made you feel appreciated and special
- Think of five people you enjoy spending time with
- Name six heroes whose stories have inspired you

How did they do?

The people who make a difference in our lives are not the ones with the most credentials, the most money, or the most awards; they are the ones who care. They have "genuine concern" for our welfare. They are our mentors, coaches, teachers, fathers and mothers. ~ Author Unknown

35

We All Need a Little Ice Cream Sometimes

L ast week, I took my grandchildren to a restaurant. My 5-year-old grandson asked if he could say grace. As we bowed our heads he said, "God is good, God is great, thank you for the food, and I would even thank you more if mom gets us ice cream for dessert, and liberty and justice for all! Amen!" Along with the laughter from the other customers nearby, I heard a woman remark, "That's what's wrong with this country. Kids today don't even know how to pray. Asking God for ice cream! Why, I never!"

Hearing this, my grandson burst into tears and asked me, "Did I do it wrong? Is God mad at me?" As I held him and assured him that he had done a terrific job, and God was certainly not mad at him, an elderly gentleman approached the table. He winked at my grandson and said, "I happen to know that God thought that was a great prayer." "Really?" my grandson asked. "Cross my heart," the man replied. Then, in a theatrical whisper, he added, "Too bad that woman never asks God for ice cream. A little ice cream is good for the soul sometimes."

Naturally, I bought my grandkids ice cream at the end of the meal. My grandson stared at his for a moment, and then did something I will remember the rest of my life. He picked up his sundae and, without a word, walked over and placed it in front of the woman. With a big smile he told her, "Here, this is for you. Ice cream is good for the soul sometimes; and my soul is good already." ~ Author Unknown?

36

The Gunnery Sergeant and the Light Bulb

O ne day a Gunnery (Gunny) Sergeant triple amputee, (lost one leg below the knee, one at the hip, and one arm below the elbow) came in with a corpsman and captain. He was truly amazing. Captain Miller had to do a rectal on him before we boarded him on an aircraft. He told the Gunny he was sorry, but he had to do it. The Gunny was cool about it and when it was done he yelled, "Hey, Doc, don't I at least get a reach-around?" Everyone in the operating room looked up, they couldn't believe what they heard, and we all chuckled. The Gunny just smiled.

"Things were looking pretty tense there for a while, and everyone was stressed." The Gunny then turned to the doctor and said, "Hey ma'am, are you okay because I need to ask you something." The doctor looked at him and the Gunny said, "How may Irishmen does it take to change a light bulb?" Her eyes filled with tears. "What did you say," she asked. The Gunny smiled and said, "it's just far too serious in here ma'am, you all have to lighten up."

He told jokes the rest of the time he was in the room. When the helicopter arrived to pick him up he waved at us with his one arm as he left the room. We felt like idiots before him. We'd been laughing the entire time he was telling jokes. Once the hatch of the aircraft closed the floodgates opened.

At the end of the long day, the doctor returned to her quarters. As she was lying for much needed rest, her roommate asked, "How many Irishmen does it take?" The doctor quietly replied, "Twenty-one: one to hold the light bulb and the other 20 to drink till the room starts spinning." ~ Author Unknown

Gentlemen, why don't you laugh? With the fearful strain that is upon me night and day, if I did not laugh, I should die. ~ Abraham Lincoln

37

A Humble Man

His name was Fleming, and he was a poor Scottish farmer. One day, while trying to make a living for his family, he heard a cry for help coming from a nearby bog. He dropped his tools and ran to the bog.

There, mired to his waist in black muck, was a terrified boy, screaming and struggling to free himself. Farmer Fleming saved the lad from what could have been a slow and terrifying death.

The next day, a fancy carriage pulled up to the Scotsman's sparse farmhouse. An elegantly dressed nobleman stepped out and introduced himself as the father of the boy Farmer Fleming had saved.

"I want to repay you," said the nobleman. "You saved my son's life."

"No, I can't accept payment for what I did," the Scottish farmer replied waving off the offer.

At that moment, the farmer's own son came to the door of the family hovel.

"Is that your son?" the nobleman asked.

"Yes," the farmer replied proudly.

"I'll make you a deal. Let me provide him with the level of education my own son will enjoy and if the lad is anything like his father, he'll no doubt grow to be a man we both will be proud of." And that he did.

Farmer Fleming's son attended the very best schools and in time, graduated from St. Mary's Hospital Medical

School in London. He went on to become known throughout the world as the noted Sir Alexander Fleming, the discoverer of Penicillin.

Years later, the same nobleman's son who was saved from the bog was stricken with pneumonia.

What saved his life this time? Penicillin.

What was the name of the nobleman? Lord Randolph Churchill.

Who was his son? Sir Winston Churchill. ~ Author Unknown

There are two ways of spreading life; to be the candle or the mirror that reflects the light. ~ Edith Wharton

Work like you don't need the money. Love like you've never been hurt. Dance like nobody's watching. Sing like nobody's listening. Live like it's heaven on earth. ~ Author Unknown

38

Your Life in Review

If you thought that the coming year would be your last, what changes would you make in your life? Who would you connect with? Would you have any regrets?

These are the kinds of questions that author Stephen Levine began to ask after years of teaching meditation and healing techniques to terminally ill patients. Levine became his own research project. He called it "the year to live." He acted as if he would be alive for only one more year. He reviewed past events that had impacted his life, both good and bad. This process inspired Levine to show his gratitude and appreciation to the many people who had touched his life in a positive way. It also helped him develop a more loving and compassionate view of the world. He found the strength to forgive the past hurts and resentments he'd been holding on to. The thought of dying allowed Levine to find the courage to commit to living a full life; to believe that nothing could hurt him now.

When you're living on borrowed time, every minute counts. It's not about taking a wild and crazy vacation to Mexico. It can be about volunteering for a literacy program if you're passionate about reading; not shaking your fist at the SUV driver who just cut you off; and making eye contact with the woman at the deli counter who slices your ham just right and wishing her a good day. ~ Author Unknown

If you could create more meaning in your life, what would you do? More to the point, what are you waiting for? ~ Author Unknown

39

Clay Balls

A man was exploring caves by the seashore. In one of the caves he found a canvas bag with dozens of hardened clay balls. It was like someone had rolled clay balls and left them out in the sun to bake. They didn't look like much, but they intrigued the man, so he took the bag out of the cave with him. As he strolled along the beach, he would throw the clay balls one at a time out into the ocean as far as he could.

He thought little about it, until he dropped one of the clay balls and it cracked open on a rock. Inside was a beautiful, precious stone!

Excited, the man started breaking open the remaining clay balls. Each contained a similar treasure. He found thousands of dollars' worth of jewels in the 20 or so clay balls he had left.

Then it struck him. He had been on the beach a long time. He had thrown maybe 50 or 60 of the clay balls with their hidden treasure into the ocean waves. Instead of thousands of dollars in treasure, he could have taken home tens of thousands but he had just thrown it away!

It's like that with people. We look at someone, maybe even ourselves, and we see the external clay vessel. It may not look like much from the outside. It isn't always beautiful or sparkling, so we discount it.

We may see that person as less important than someone more beautiful or stylish or well known or wealthy, but we have not taken the time to find the treasure hidden inside that person. There is a treasure in each and every one of us. If we take the time to get to know that person, and if we ask God to show us that person the way He sees them, then the clay begins to chip away and the brilliant gem begins to shine forth.

May we not come to the end of our lives and find out that we have thrown away a fortune in friendships because the gems were hidden in bits of clay. May we see the people in our world as God sees them.

I am so blessed by the gems of friendship I have with you. Thank you for looking beyond my clay vessel.
~ Author Unknown

Appreciate every single friends you have, especially your friendships. Life is too short and friends are too few.
~ Author Unknown

Enjoy life; it's not a dress rehearsal. You only get one shot to make it right. ~ Joseph Shusko

40

Eddie Rickenbacker

It happens every Friday evening, almost without fail, when the sun resembles a giant orange and is starting to dip into the blue ocean. Old Ed comes strolling along the beach to his favorite pier. Clutched in his bony hand is a bucket of shrimp. Ed walks out to the end of the pier, where it seems he almost has the world to himself. The glow of the setting sun is a golden bronze. Everybody's gone, except for a few joggers on the beach. Standing out on the end of the pier, Ed is alone with his thoughts and his bucket of shrimp.

Before long, however, he is no longer alone.

Up in the sky a thousand white dots come screeching and squawking, winging their way toward that lanky frame standing on the end of the pier. Before long dozens of seagulls have enveloped him, their wings fluttering and flapping wildly. Ed stands there tossing shrimp to the hungry birds. As he does, if you listen closely, you can hear him say with a smile, "Thank you. Thank you." In a few short minutes the bucket is empty. But Ed doesn't leave. He stands there lost in thought, as though transported to another time and place.

Invariably, one of the gulls lands on his sea-bleached, weather-beaten hat; an old military hat he's been wearing for years. When he finally turns around and begins to walk back toward the beach, a few of the birds hop along the pier with him until he gets to the stairs and then they too fly away.

Old Ed quietly makes his way down to the end of the beach and on home. If you were sitting there on the pier with your fishing line in the water, Ed might seem like "a funny old duck," as my dad used to say. Or, "a guy that's a sandwich shy of a picnic," as my kids might say. To onlookers, he's just another old codger, lost in his own weird world, feeding the seagulls with a bucket full of shrimp. To the onlooker, rituals can look either very strange or very empty. They can seem altogether unimportant; maybe even a lot of nonsense.

Old folks often do strange things, at least in the eyes of boomers and busters. Most of them would probably write old Ed off. That's too bad. They'd do well to know him better. His full name is Eddie Rickenbacker and he was World War II hero.

On one of his flying missions across the Pacific, he and his seven-member crew went down. Miraculously, all of the men survived, crawled out of their plane, and climbed into a life raft. For 24 days, Rickenbacker, the Army Captain Hans C. Adamson, his friend and business partner, and the rest of the crewmen drifted in life rafts at sea. Rickenbacker was still suffering somewhat from his earlier airplane crash and Capt. Adamson sustained serious injuries during the ditching. The other crewmen in the B-17 were hurt to varying degrees.

The crewmen's food supply ran out after three days. Then, on the eighth day, a seagull landed on Rickenbacker's head. He warily and cautiously captured it, and then the survivors meticulously divided it into equal parts and used part of it for fishing bait. They lived on sporadic rain water that fell and similar food "miracles".

Rickenbacker assumed leadership, encouraging and browbeating the others to keep their spirits up. One crewman, Alexander Kaczmarczyk of the USAAF, died and was buried at sea. The U.S. Army Air Forces and the U.S. Navy's patrol planes planned to abandon the search for the lost B-17 crewmen after just over two weeks, but Rickenbacker's wife persuaded them to extend it another week. The services agreed to do so. Once again, the newspapers and radio broadcasts reported that Rickenbacker was dead.

A U.S. Navy patrol OS2U-3 Kingfisher float-plane piloted by Lieutenant William F. Eddie, USN, spotted and rescued the survivors on November 13, 1942 off the coast of Nukufetau near the Samoa Islands. All were suffering from exposure, sunburn, dehydration and near-starvation. Eddie was awarded the Navy's Air Medal for his actions.

Eddie Rickenbacker lived many years beyond that ordeal, but he never forgot the sacrifice of that first lifesaving seagull. And he never stopped saying, "Thank you." That's why rumor has it that almost every Friday night he would walk to the end of the pier with a bucket full of shrimp and a heart full of gratitude. ~ Actual Author Unknown but mentioned in many sources.

41

Rainbow Bridge

Just this side of heaven is a place called Rainbow Bridge. When an animal dies that has been especially close to someone here, that pet goes to Rainbow Bridge. There are meadows and hills for all of our special friends so they can run and play together. There is plenty of food, water and sunshine, and our friends are warm and comfortable.

All the animals that had been ill and old are restored to health and vigor. Those who were hurt or maimed are made whole and strong again, just as we remember them in our dreams of days and times gone by.

The animals are happy and content, except for one small thing; they each miss someone very special to them who had to be left behind. They all run and play together, but the day comes when one suddenly stops and looks into the distance. His bright eyes are intent. His eager body quivers. Suddenly, he begins to run from the group, flying over the green grass, his legs carrying him faster and faster. You have been spotted, and when you and your special friend finally meet, you cling together in joyous reunion, never to be parted again. The happy kisses rain upon your face; your hands again caress the beloved head, and you look once more into the trusting eyes of your pet, so long gone from your life but never absent from your heart. Then you cross Rainbow Bridge together. ~ Author Unknown

42

If It Should Be

If it should be that I grow weak
And pain should keep me from my sleep,
Then you must do what must be done,
For the last battle cannot be won.

You will be sad, I understand.
Don't let your grief then stay your hand.
For this day, more than all the rest,
Your love for me must stand the test.

We've had so many happy years.
What is to come can hold no fears.
You'd not want me to suffer so;
The time has come – please let me go.

Take me where my need they'll tend,
And please stay with me till the end.
Hold me firm and speak to me,
Until my eyes no longer see.

I know in time that you will see
The kindness that you did for me.
Although my tail its last has waved,
From pain and suffering I've been saved.

Please do not grief – it must be you
Who had this painful thing to do.
We've been so close, we two, these years;
Don't let your heart hold back its tears. ~ Anonymous

43

I Hate When My Eyes Sweat

I just wanted to get the day over with and go down to Smokey's for a cold soda. Sneaking a look at my watch, I saw that the time was 1655. Five minutes to go before the cemetery gates are closed for the day. Full dress was hot in the August sun. Oklahoma summertime was as bad as ever – the heat and humidity at the same level – both too high.

I saw the car pull into the drive, a 1969 or 1970 model Cadillac Deville, and it looked factory-new. It pulled into the parking lot at a snail's pace. An old woman got out so slowly I thought she was almost paralyzed. She had a cane and a sheaf of flowers – about four or five bunches as best I could tell. I couldn't help myself. The thought came unwanted, and left a slightly bitter taste: "She's going to spend an hour, and for this old soldier, my hip hurts like hell and I'm ready to get out of here right now!"

But for this day, my duty was to assist anyone coming in. Kevin would lock the "In" gate and if I could hurry the old gal along, we might make it to Smokey's in time.

I broke post attention. My hip made gritty noises when I took the first step and the pain went up a notch. I must have made a real military sight: middle-aged man with a small pot gut and half a limp, in Marine full-dress uniform, which had lost its razor crease about thirty minutes after I began the watch at the cemetery.

I stopped in front of her, halfway up the walk. She looked up at me with an old woman's squint.

"Ma'am, may I assist you in any way?" She took long enough to answer.

"Yes, son. Can you carry these flowers? I seem to be moving a tad slow these days."

"My pleasure, ma'am." Well, it wasn't too much of a lie.

She looked again. "Marine, where were you stationed?"

"Vietnam, ma'am," I replied. "Ground-pounder. 1969 to 1971."

She looked at me closer. "Wounded in action, I see. Well done, Marine. I'll be as quick as I can."

I lied a little bigger: "No hurry, ma'am." She smiled and winked at me.

"Son, I'm 85-years-old and I can tell a lie from a long way off. Let's get this done. Might be the last time I can do this. My name's Joanne Wieserman, and I've a few Marines I'd like to see one more time."

"Yes, Ma'am. At your service." She headed for the World War I section, stopping at a stone. She picked one of the flowers out of my arm and laid it on top of the stone. She murmured something I couldn't quite make out. The name on the marble was Donald S. Davidson, USMC: France 1918.

She turned away and made a straight line for the World War II section, stopping at one stone. I saw a tear slowly tracking its way down her cheek. She put a bunch on a stone; the name was Stephen X. Davidson, USMC, 1943.

She went up the row a ways and laid another bunch on a stone, Stanley J. Wieserman, USMC, 1944.

She paused for a second. "Two more, son, and we'll be done." I almost didn't say anything, but, "Yes, ma'am. Take your time." She looked confused.

"Where's the Vietnam section, son? I seem to have lost my way." I pointed with my chin. "That way, ma'am." "Oh!" she chuckled quietly. "Son, me and old age ain't too friendly."

She headed down the walk where I pointed. She stopped at a couple of stones before she found the ones she wanted. She placed a bunch on Larry Wieserman, USMC, 1968, and the last on Darrel Wieserman, USMC, 1970.

She stood there and murmured a few words I still couldn't make out.

"OK, son, I'm finished. Get me back to my car and you can go home."

"Yes, ma'am. If I may ask, were those your kinfolk?"

She paused. "Yes, Donald Davidson was my father, Stephen was my uncle, Stanley was my husband, Larry and Darrel were our sons. All killed in action, all Marines." She stopped. Whether she had finished, or couldn't finish, I don't know.

She made her way to her car, slowly and painfully.

I waited for a polite distance to come between us and then double-timed it over to Kevin, waiting by the car. "Get to the 'Out' gate quick. I have something I've got to do." Kevin started to say something but saw the look I gave him. He broke the rules to get us there down the service road. We beat her. She hadn't made it around the rotunda yet.

"Kevin, stand at attention next to the gatepost. Follow my lead." I humped it across the drive to the other post.

When the Cadillac came puttering around from the hedges and began the short straight traverse to the gate, I called in my best gunny's voice: "Tehen Hut! Present Haaaarms!"

I have to hand it to Kevin; he never blinked an eye – full dress attention and a salute that would make his drill instructor proud.

She drove through that gate with two old worn-out Marines giving her a send-off she deserved, for service rendered to her country, and for knowing duty, honor and sacrifice. I am not sure, but I think I saw a salute returned from that Cadillac.

Instead of "The End," just think of "Taps." ~ Author Unknown

As a final thought on my part, let me share a favorite prayer: "Lord, keep our servicemen and women safe, whether they serve at home or overseas. Hold them in your loving hands and protect them as they protect us."

Let's all keep those currently serving and those who have gone before in our thoughts. They are the reason for the many freedoms we enjoy. "In God We Trust."

Sorry about your monitor; it made mine blurry too! If we ever forget that we're one nation under God, then we will be a nation gone under! ~ Author Unknown

When a person realizes their littleness, their greatness can appear. ~ H.G. Wells

44

Old Man

As I came out of the supermarket that sunny day, pushing my cart of groceries toward my car, I saw an old man with the hood of his car up and a lady sitting inside the car, with the door open. The old man was looking at the engine. I put my groceries away in my car and continued to watch the old gentleman from about 25 feet away. I saw a young man in his early twenties with a grocery bag in his arm, walking toward the old man. The old gentleman saw him coming too and took a few steps toward him. I saw the old gentleman point to his open hood and say something. The young man put his grocery bag into what looked like a brand new Cadillac Escalade and then turn back to the old man and I heard him yell at the old gentleman saying, "You shouldn't even be allowed to drive a car at your age." And then with a wave of his hand, he got in his car and peeled rubber out of the parking lot.

I saw the old gentleman pull out his handkerchief and mop his brow as he went back to his car and again looked at the engine. He then went to his wife and spoke with her and appeared to tell her it would be okay.

I had seen enough and I approached the old man. He saw me coming and stood straight and as I got near him I said, "Looks like you're having a problem." He smiled sheepishly and quietly nodded his head.

I looked under the hood myself and knew that whatever the problem was, it was beyond me. Looking around I saw a gas station up the road and told the old man that I would be right back.

I drove to the station and went inside and saw three attendants working on cars. I approached one of them and related the problem the old man had with his car and offered to pay them if they could follow me back down to help him. The old man had pushed the heavy car under the shade of a tree and appeared to be comforting his wife. When he saw us he straightened up and thanked me for my help.

As the mechanics diagnosed the problem (overheated engine) I spoke with the old gentleman. When I shook hands with him earlier he had noticed my Marine Corps ring and had commented about it, telling me that he had been a Marine too. I nodded and asked the usual question, "What outfit did you serve with?" He had mentioned that he served with the first Marine Division at Tarawa, Saipan, Iwo Jima and Guadalcanal. He had hit all the big ones and retired from the Corps after the war was over.

As we talked we heard the car engine come on and saw the mechanics lower the hood. They came over to us as the old man reached for his wallet, but was stopped by me and I told him I would just put the bill on my AAA card. He still reached for the wallet and handed me a card that I assumed had his name and address on it and I stuck it in my pocket.

We all shook hands all around again and I said my goodbyes to his wife. I then told the two mechanics that I would follow them back up to the station. Once at the station I told them that they had interrupted their own jobs to come along with me and help the old man. I said I wanted to pay for the help, but they refused to charge me. One of them pulled out a card from his pocket looking exactly like the card the old man had given to me.

Both of the men told me then, that they were Marine Corps Reservists. Once again we shook hands all around and as I was leaving, one of them told me I should look at the card the old man had given to me. I said I would and drove off.

For some reason I had gone about two blocks when I pulled over and took the card out of my pocket and looked at it for a long, long, time. The name of the old gentleman was on the card in golden leaf and under his name. "Congressional Medal of Honor Society."

I sat there motionless looking at the card and reading it over and over. I looked up from the card and smiled to no one but myself and marveled that on this day, four Marines had all come together, because one of us needed help. He was an old man all right, but it felt good to have stood next to greatness and courage and an honor to have been in his presence.

America is not at war. The U.S Military is at war, America is at the Mall. If you don't stand behind our troops, PLEASE feel free to stand in front of them!
~ Author Unknown

45

The Power of Encouragement

Dante Gabriel Rossetti, the famous 19th century poet and artist, was once approached by an elderly man. The old fellow had some sketches and drawings that he wanted Rossetti to look at and tell him if they were any good, or if they at least showed potential talent.

Rossetti looked them over carefully. After the first few, he knew that they were worthless and didn't show the least sign of artistic talent. But Rossetti was a kind man, and he told the elderly man as gently as possible that the pictures were without much value and showed little talent. He was sorry, but he could not lie to the man. The visitor was disappointed, but seemed to expect Rossetti's judgment.

He then apologized for taking up Rossetti's time, but would he just look at a few more drawings – these done by a young art student? Rossetti looked over the second batch of sketches and immediately became enthusiastic over the talent they revealed.

"These," he said, "Oh, these are good. This young student has great talent. He should be given every help and encouragement in his career as an artist. He has a great future if he will work hard and stick to it."

Rossetti could see that the old fellow was deeply moved. "Who is this fine young artist?" he asked. "Your son?" "No," said the old man sadly. "It is me, 40 years ago.

If only I had heard your praise then! For you see, I got discouraged and gave up too soon." ~ Author Unknown

46

The Seed

Asuccessful business man was growing old and knew it was time to choose a successor to take over his business. Instead of choosing one of his directors or his children, he decided to do something different. He called all the young executives in his company together.

He said, "It is time for me to step down and choose the next CEO. I have decided to choose one of you." The young executives were shocked, but the boss continued. "I am going to give each one of you a SEED today – one very special SEED. I want you to plant the seed, water it, and come back here one year from today with what you have grown from the seed I have given you. Then I will judge the plants you bring and the one I choose will be the next CEO."

One young executive, Jim, was there that day and he, like the others, received a seed. He went home and excitedly told his wife the story. She helped him get a pot, soil and compost and he planted the seed. Every day, he would water it and check to see if it had grown. After about three weeks, some of the other executives began to talk about their seeds and the plants that were beginning to grow.

Jim kept checking his seed, but nothing ever grew. Three weeks, four weeks, five weeks went by and still nothing. The others would talk about their plants, but Jim didn't have a plant and he felt like a failure. Six months went by and still nothing grew in Jim's pot. He just knew he had killed his seed. Everyone else had trees and tall plants, but he had nothing. Jim didn't say anything to his colleagues, however. He just kept watering and fertilizing the soil. He desperately wanted the seed to grow.

A year finally went by and the day arrived when all the young executives were to bring their plants to the CEO for inspection. Jim told his wife that he wasn't going to take an empty pot, but she asked him to be honest about what happened. Jim felt sick to his stomach – it was going to be the most embarrassing moment of his life – but he knew his wife was right. He took his empty pot to the board room. When Jim arrived, he was amazed at the variety of plants grown by the other executives. They were beautiful and in all shapes and sizes. Jim put his empty pot on the floor and many of his colleagues laughed; a few even felt sorry for him!

When the CEO arrived, he surveyed the room and greeted his young executives. Jim just tried to hide in the back.

"My, what great plants, trees and flowers you have grown," said the CEO. "Today one of you will be appointed the next CEO!"

All of a sudden, the CEO spotted Jim at the back of the room with his empty pot. He ordered the financial director to bring him to the front. Jim was terrified. He thought, "The CEO knows I'm a failure! Maybe he will have me fired!"

When Jim got to the front, the CEO asked him what had happened to his seed. Jim told him the story.

The CEO asked everyone to sit down except Jim. He looked at Jim, and then announced to the young executives, "Behold, your next Chief Executive Officer! His name is Jim!"

Jim couldn't believe it. Jim couldn't even grow his seed. "How could he be the new CEO?" The others said.

Then the CEO said, "One year ago today, I gave everyone in this room a seed. I told you to take the seed, plant it, water it, and bring it back to me today. But I gave you all boiled seeds; they were dead so it was not possible for them to grow. All of you, except Jim, have brought me trees, plants and flowers. When you found that the seed would not grow, you substituted another seed for the one I gave you. Jim was the only one with the courage and honesty to bring me a pot with my seed in it. Therefore, he is the one who will be the new Chief Executive Officer." ~ Author Unknown

- If you plant honesty, you will reap trust.
- If you plant goodness, you will reap friends.
- If you plant humility, you will reap greatness.
- If you plant perseverance, you will reap contentment.
- If you plant consideration, you will reap perspective.
- If you plant hard work, you will reap success.
  ~ Author Unknown

May you continue to plant seeds of integrity so that you can reap all the great things that life has to offer.
~ Author Unknown

Even a slow walker will arrive. ~ African Proverb

47

Seven Ways to Live a Better Life

1. Show appreciation
2. Reach out and connect with others
3. Work on relationships
4. Find role models
5. Smile, often
6. Focus on positive people
7. Build your own support network
   ~ Author Unknown

48

You Don't Have To Be Big To Make a Difference

A Native American folktale from the Anishnabe people tells of a great river that was filled with many fish and such sweet water that many of the animals came to its banks to drink.

When a giant moose heard about the river he went there to drink too. But the moose was so big and he drank so much that the water began to dry up. The beavers were the first to worry. If the river disappeared what would become of their lodges? The muskrats were worried about how they would live without the river. The fish were also worried. They could not survive on land like other creatures. The water was their home.

All of the animals gathered together to brainstorm a way to drive away the moose. But he was so big that even the bear was afraid to approach him.

Then the fly said, "I'll do it. I'll make the moose leave." The animals began to laugh. "How could one little fly scare a giant moose?"

But the fly ignored their jeers and waited for the moose to return to the river for a drink. Once the moose showed up, the fly went to work.

First the fly bit the moose on the leg causing him to stamp his hooves into the ground. Each time the moose did this, the ground sank and more water poured forth.

Then the fly began to bite the moose all over. The moose snorted and ran trying to avoid the annoying fly. But it was of no use. The fly would not stop.

Finally, the moose became so upset that he ran from the river and never returned there to drink. The fly was quite proud of his achievement.

"Even the small can fight the strong," he boasted to the other animals, "If they use their brains to think." ~ Author Unknown

Be who God meant you to be an you will set the world on fire. ~ Catherine of Siena

49

Nails in the Fence

There once was a little boy who had a bad temper. His father gave him a bag of nails and a tiny hammer and told him that every time he lost his temper, he must hammer a nail into the back of the fence.

By the end of the first day, the boy had driven 37 nails into the fence. Over the next few weeks, as he learned to control his anger, the number of nails hammered daily gradually dwindled down. He discovered it was easier to hold his temper than to drive those nails into the fence.

Finally the day came when the boy didn't lose his temper at all. He told his father about it and the father suggested that the boy now pull out one nail for each day that he was able to hold his temper.

The days passed and the young boy was finally able to tell his father that all the nails were gone. The father took his son by the hand and led him to the fence. He said, "You have done well, my son, but look at the holes in the fence. The fence will never be the same. When you say things in anger, they leave a scar just like this one."

You can put a knife in a man and draw it out. But it won't matter how many times you say "I'm sorry," the wound will still be there. A verbal wound is as bad as a physical one.

Remember that friends are very rare jewels. They make you smile and encourage you to succeed. They lend an ear, they share words of praise and they always want to open their hearts to us. Please forgive me if I have ever left a 'hole' in your fence. ~ Author Unknown

50

Listen Has the Same Letters as Silent

Before refrigerators, people used icehouses to preserve their food. Icehouses had thick walls, no windows and a tightly fitted door.

In winter, when streams and lakes were frozen, large blocks of ice were cut, hauled to the icehouses and covered with sawdust. Often the ice would last well into the summer.

A man once lost a valuable watch while working in an icehouse. He searched diligently for it, carefully raking through the sawdust, but didn't find it. His fellow workers also looked, but their efforts, too, proved futile.

A small boy who heard about the fruitless search slipped into the icehouse during the noon hour and soon emerged with the watch. Amazed, the men asked him how he found it. "I closed the door," the boy replied, "laid down in the sawdust, and kept very still. Soon I heard the watch ticking."

Often the question is not whether God is speaking, but whether we are being still enough, and quiet enough, to hear. ~ Author Unknown

When the student is ready, the master appears.
~ Buddhist Proverb

51

Two Wolves

One evening an old Cherokee told his grandson about a battle that goes on inside people. He said, "My son, the battle is between two wolves inside us all. One is Evil – It is anger, envy, jealousy, sorrow, regret, greed, arrogance, self-pity, guilt, resentment, inferiority, lies, false pride, superiority and ego. The other is Good – It is joy, peace, love, hope, serenity, humility, kindness, benevolence, empathy, generosity, truth, compassion and faith."

The grandson thought about it for a minute and then asked his grandfather: "Which wolf wins?"

The old Cherokee simply replied, "The one you feed."

~ Author Unknown (Cherokee Legend)

The wolf loses his teeth, but not his inclination.

~ Spanish Proverb

52

God Lives Under The Bed

I envy Kevin. My brother, Kevin, thinks God lives under his bed. At least that's what I heard him say one night.

He was praying out loud in his dark bedroom, and I stopped to listen. "Are you there, God?" he said? "Where are you? Oh, I see. Under the bed." I giggled softly and tiptoed off to my own room.

Kevin's unique perspectives are often a source of amusement. But, that night something else lingered long after the humor. I realized for the first time the very different world Kevin lives in. He was born 30 years ago and is mentally disabled as a result of difficulties during labor. Apart from his size (he's 6-foot 2-inch and 220 pounds); there are few ways in which he is an adult. He reasons and communicates with the capabilities of a 7-year-old, and he always will.

He will probably always believe that God lives under his bed, that Santa Claus is the one who fills the space under our tree every Christmas and that airplanes stay up in the sky because angels carry them.

I remember wondering if Kevin realizes he is different. Is he ever dissatisfied with his monotonous life? He's up before dawn each day and heads off to work at a workshop for the disabled. He returns home in the afternoon to walk our cocker spaniel, enjoy dinner which always includes a side of his favorite macaroni-and-cheese, and later heads to bed to pray and sleep. variation in the entire scheme is the day he d' he hovers excitedly over the washing machin mother with her newborn child. He does not seem dissatisfied.

He's happy when he lopes out to the bus every morning at 7:05 a.m., eager for a day of simple work. He wrings his hands excitedly while the water boils for his macaroni-and-cheese on the stove before dinner, and he stays up late twice a week to gather our dirty laundry for his next day's laundry chores. And Saturdays – oh, the bliss of Saturdays! That's the day my dad takes Kevin to the airport to have a soft drink, watch the planes land, and speculate loudly on the destination of each passenger inside.

"That one's going' to Chi-car-go!" Kevin shouts as he claps his hands. His anticipation is so great he can hardly sleep on Friday nights.

And so goes his world of daily rituals and weekend field trips. He doesn't know what it means to be discontent. His life is simple.

He will never know the entanglements of wealth or power, and he does not care what brand of clothing he wears or what kind of food he eats. His needs have always been met, and he never worries that one day they may not be. His hands are diligent. Kevin is happiest as when he is working. When he unloads the dishwasher or vacuums the carpet, his heart is completely in it.

He does not shrink from a job when it is begun, and he does not leave a job until it is finished. But when his tasks are done, Kevin knows how to relax. He is not obsessed with his work or the work of others. His heart is pure. He still believes everyone tells the truth, promises must be kept, and when you are wrong, you apologize instead of argue. Free from pride and unconcerned with appearances, Kevin is not afraid to cry when he is hurt, angry or sorry. He is always transparent, always sincere. And he trusts God.

Not confined by intellectual reasoning, when he comes to Christ he comes as a child. Kevin seems to know God – to really be friends with Him in a way that is difficult for an 'educated' person to grasp. God seems like his closest companion. In my moments of doubt and frustrations with my Christianity, I envy the security Kevin has in his simple faith.

It is then that I am most willing to admit that he has some divine knowledge that rises above my mortal questions. It is then I realize that perhaps he is not the one with the handicap. I am. My obligations, my fear, my pride, my circumstances – they all become disabilities when I do not trust them to God's care. Who knows if Kevin comprehends things I can never learn? After all, he has spent his whole life in that kind of innocence, praying after dark and soaking up the goodness and love of God. And one day, when the mysteries of heaven are opened, and we are all amazed at how close God really is to our hearts, I'll realize that God heard the simple prayers of a boy who believed that God lived under his bed. Kevin won't be surprised at all!

Friends are Angels who lift us to our feet when wings have trouble remembering how to fly. ~ Author Unknown

53

Sleeping When the Wind Blows

Years ago a farmer owned land along the Atlantic seacoast. He constantly advertised for hired hands. Most people were reluctant to work on farms along the Atlantic. They dreaded the awful storms that raged across the Atlantic, wreaking havoc on the buildings and crops. As the farmer interviewed applicants for the job, he received a steady stream of refusals. Finally, a short, thin man, well past middle age, approached the farmer. "Are you a good farm hand?" the farmer asked him. "Well, I can sleep when the wind blows," answered the little man. Although puzzled by this answer, the farmer, desperate for help, hired him. The little man worked well around the farm, busy from dawn to dusk, and the farmer felt satisfied with the man's work. Then one night the wind howled loudly in from offshore. Jumping out of bed, the farmer grabbed a lantern and rushed next door to the hired hand's sleeping quarters. He shook the little man and yelled, "Get up! A storm is coming! Tie things down before they blow away!" The little man rolled over in bed and said firmly, "No sir. I told you, I can sleep when the wind blows." Enraged by the response, the farmer was tempted to fire him on the spot. Instead, he hurried outside to prepare for the storm. To his amazement, he discovered that all of the haystacks had been covered with tarpaulins. The cows were in the barn, the chickens were in the coops, and the doors were barred. The shutters were tightly secured. Everything was tied down. Nothing could blow away. The

farmer then understood what his hired hand meant, so he returned to his bed to also sleep while the wind blew.
~ Author Unknown

54

Chancing One's Arm

There is an ancient door on display in St. Patrick's cathedral in Dublin, Ireland. The roughhewn door has a rectangular hole hacked out in its center. It is called the "Door of Reconciliation," and gives rise to the Irish expression of "chancing one's arm."

In 1492, two prominent Irish families, the Ormands and the Kildares, were in the midst of a bitter feud. As the feud grew and turned into an all-out fight, the Earl of Ormand was besieged by the Earl of Kildare.

The Earl of Ormand, his family and his followers took refuge in the chapter house of St. Patrick's cathedral and bolted themselves in.

However, as the siege wore on, the Earl of Kildare concluded the feuding was foolish. Here were two families worshiping the same God, in the same church, living in the same country, trying to kill each other.

So Kildare called out to the Earl of Ormand and pledged that he would not seek revenge or indulge in villainy; he wanted the Ormands to come out and the feud to be over. But the Earl of Ormand was convinced that it was a scheme full of treachery and refused to come out of the cathedral.

So Kildare grabbed his spear, chopped a hole in the door with it, and thrust his hand through. There was a tense moment until his hand was grasped by another hand inside the church.

The door was opened and the two men embraced, thus ending the family feud. From Kildare's noble gesture came the expression, "chancing one's arm."

Hopefully, these days will be marked by God's people "chancing one's arm." There is always the chance that the hand will be cut off, but there is also the chance that it will be grasped and that an embrace will follow.

May God give us courage and grace.

~ Author Unknown

55

This is Good

The story is told of a king in Africa who had a close friend with whom he grew up. The friend had a habit of looking at every situation that ever occurred in his life (positive or negative) and remarking, "This is good!"

One day the king and his friend were out on a hunting expedition. The friend would load and prepare the guns for the king. The friend had apparently done something wrong in preparing one of the guns. After taking the gun from his friend, the king fired it and his thumb was blown off. Examining the situation, the friend remarked as usual, "This is good!" To which the king replied, "No, this is not good!" and proceeded to send his friend to jail.

About a year later, the king was hunting in an area that he should have known to stay clear of. Cannibals captured him and took him to their village. They tied his hands, stacked some wood, set up a stake and bound him to the stake. As they approached to set fire to the wood, they noticed that the king was missing a thumb. They were superstitious and never ate anyone who was less than whole. So they quickly untied the king and sent him on his way.

As he returned home, he was reminded of the event that had taken his thumb and felt remorse for his treatment of his friend. He went immediately to the jail to speak with his friend. "You were right," he said, "it was good that my thumb was blown off." He proceeded to tell the friend all that had just happened.

"And so, I am very sorry for sending you to jail for so long," said the king. "It was bad for me to do this."

"No," his friend replied, "This is good!"

"What do you mean, 'This is good'? How could it be good that I sent my friend to jail for a year?"

"If I had not been in jail, I would have been with you."
~ Author Unknown

A friend thinks of you when all other are thinking of themselves. ~ Author Unknown

56

Shirley and Marcy

A mom was concerned about her kindergarten son walking to school. He didn't want his mother to walk with him. She wanted to give him the feeling that he had some independence but yet know that he was safe.

So she had an idea of how to handle it. She asked a neighbor if she would please follow him to school in the mornings, staying at a distance, so he probably wouldn't notice her.

The neighbor said that since she was up early with her toddler anyway, it would be a good way for them to get some exercise as well so she agreed.

The next school day, the neighbor and her little girl set out following behind Timmy as he walked to school with another neighbor girl. She did this for the whole week.

As the two walked and chatted, kicking stones and twigs, Timmy's little friend noticed the same lady was following them as she seemed to do every day all week. Finally she said to Timmy, "Have you noticed that lady following us to school all week? Do you know her?"

Timmy nonchalantly replied, "Yeah, I know who she is."

The little girl said, "Well, who is she?"

"That's just Shirley Goodness," Timmy replied, "and her daughter, Marcy."

"Shirley Goodness? Who the heck is she and why is she following us?"

"Well," Timmy explained, "every night my Mom makes me say the 23rd Psalm with my prayers, 'cuz she worries about me so much. And in the Psalm, it says, 'Shirley Goodness and Marcy shall follow me all the days of my life', so I guess I'll just have to get used to it!"

May Shirley Goodness and Marcy be with you today and always. ~ Author Unknown

The Lord blesses you and keeps you; the Lord makes His face to shine upon you, and be gracious unto you; the Lord lifts His countenance upon you, and gives you peace. ~ Author Unknown

Remember that the faith to move mountains always carries a pick. ~ Author Unknown

57

It's Not About You

A fascinating study on the principle of the Golden Rule was conducted by Bernard Rimland, director of the Institute for Child Behavior Research. Rimland found "The happiest people are those who help others."

Each person involved in the study was asked to list ten people he or she knew best and to label them as happy or not happy.

Then they were to go through the list again and label each one as selfish or unselfish, using the following definition of selfishness: "a stable tendency to devote one's time and resources to one's own interests and welfare – an unwillingness to inconvenience one's self for others."

In categorizing the results, Rimland found all of the people labeled happy were also labeled unselfish.

He wrote that those "whose activities are devoted to bringing themselves happiness ... are far less likely to be happy than those whose efforts are devoted to making others happy."

Rimland concluded: "Do unto others as you would have them do unto you." ~ Author Unknown

Whether you are leading a Battalion of Marines or participating in a marriage relationship, it is better to give than to receive. ~ Author Unknown

Be patient with a bad neighbor; He may move or face misfortune. ~ Egyptian Proverb

Treat every day as if it were your last. Treat everybody else as if they were you. ~ Author Unknown

58

Eagles in the Storm

Did you know an eagle knows when a storm is approaching long before it breaks? The eagle will fly to a high spot and wait for the winds to come. When the storm hits, it sets its wings so that the wind will pick it up and lift it above the storm. While the storm rages below, the eagle is soaring above it.

The eagle does not escape the storm. It simply uses the storm to lift it higher. It rises on the winds that bring the storm.

When the storms of life come upon us – and all of us will experience them – we can rise above them by setting our minds and our beliefs toward God. The storms do not have to overcome us. We can allow God's power to lift us above them.

God enables us to ride the winds of the storm that bring sickness, tragedy, failure and disappointment in our lives. We can soar above the storm.

Remember, it is not the burdens of life that weigh us down; it is how we handle them. ~ Author Unknown

No one ever sized up humans so well than the fellow who invented the pencil eraser. ~ Author Unknown

59

The Buzzard, the Bat
and the Bumblebee

If you put a buzzard in a 6 feet by 8 feet square pen that's entirely open at the top, the bird, in spite of its ability to fly, will be an absolute prisoner. A buzzard always begins a flight from the ground with a run of 10 or 12 feet. Without the space to run it will not even attempt to fly, but will remain a prisoner for life in a small jail with no top.

The ordinary bat that flies around at night, a remarkably nimble creature in the air, cannot take off from a level place. If it is placed on the floor or flat ground, all it can do is shuffle about helplessly and, no doubt, painfully, until it reaches some slight elevation from which it can throw itself into the air. Then, at once, it takes off like a flash.

A bumblebee, if dropped into an open tumbler will stay there until it dies unless it is taken out. It never sees the means of escape at the top, but persists in trying to find some way out through the sides near the bottom. It will seek a way where none exists, until it completely destroys itself.

In many ways, there are lots of people like the buzzard, the bat and the bee. They are struggling about with all their problems and frustrations, not realizing that the answer is right there above them. ~ Author Unknown

60

The Cleaning Lady

During my second month of college, our professor gave us a pop quiz. I was a conscientious student and had breezed through the questions until I read the last one:

"What is the first name of the woman who cleans the school?" Surely this was some kind of joke. I had seen the cleaning woman several times. She was tall, dark-haired and in her 50's, but how would I know her name?

I handed in my paper, leaving the last question blank. Just before class ended, one student asked if the last question would count towards our quiz grade.

"Absolutely," said the professor. "In your careers, you will meet many people. All are significant. They deserve your attention and care, even if all you do is smile and say "hello."

I've never forgotten that lesson or the cleaning lady's name, Dorothy. ~ Author Unknown

All men are created equal. ~ Philip Mazzei

61

Giving When It Counts

Many years ago, when I worked as a volunteer at a hospital, I got to know a little 8-year-old girl named Liz who was suffering from a rare and serious disease. Her only chance of recovery appeared to be a blood transfusion from her 5-year-old brother, who had miraculously survived the same disease and had developed the antibodies needed to combat the illness. The doctor explained the situation to her little brother, and asked the little boy if he would be willing to give his blood to his sister.

I saw him hesitate for only a moment before taking a deep breath and saying, "Yes I'll do it if it will save her."

As the transfusion progressed, he laid in bed next to his sister and smiled, as we all did, seeing the color returning to her cheek. Then his face grew pale and his smile faded.

He looked up at the doctor and asked with a trembling voice, "Will I start to die right away."

Being young, the little boy had misunderstood the doctor; he thought he was going to have to give his sister all of his blood in order to save her.

The best thing you can give someone is a chance.

~ Author Unknown

Work like you don't need the money, love like you've never been hurt and dance like you do when nobody's watching. ~ Satchel Paige

62

Sand and Stone

Two friends were walking through the desert. During some point of the journey they had an argument and one friend slapped the other one across the face. The one who got slapped was hurt, but, without saying anything, wrote in the sand, "TODAY MY BEST FRIEND SLAPPED ME IN THE FACE."

They kept walking until they found an oasis, where they decided to take a bath. The one who had been slapped got stuck in the mire and started drowning, but his friend saved him. After the friend recovered from the near drowning he carved on a stone, "TODAY MY BEST FRIEND SAVED MY LIFE."

The friend who had slapped and saved his best friend asked him, "After I hurt you, you wrote in the sand and now, you write on a stone, why?"

The other friend replied, "When someone hurts us, we should write it down in sand where winds of forgiveness can erase it away. But, when someone does something good for us, we must engrave it in stone where no wind can ever erase it."

Learn to write your hurts in the sand and to carve your benefits in stone. ~ Author Unknown

63

Basic Math

Here is a little something someone sent me that is indisputable mathematical logic. It also made me laugh out loud.

This is a strictly mathematical viewpoint. It goes like this:

What makes 100%?

What does it mean to give more than 100%?

Ever wonder about those people who say they are giving more than 100%?

Have you attended a meeting where someone asked you to give more than 100%?

How about achieving 103%?

What makes up 100% in life?

Here is a little mathematical formula that might help you answer these questions:

If A B C D E F G H I J K L M N O P Q R S T U V W X Y Z is represented as:

1 2 3 4 5 6 7 8 9 10 11 12 13 14 15 16 17 18 19 20 21 22 23 24 25 26.

Then H-A-R-D-W-O-R-K is 8+1+18+4+23+15+18+11 = 98%

And K-N-O-W-L-E-D-G-E is 11+14+15+23+12+5+4+7+5 = 96%

But A-T-T-I-T-U-D-E is 1+20+20+9+20+21+4+5 = 100%

And B-U-L-L-S-H-I-T is 2+21+12+12+19+8+9+20 = 103%

So one can conclude with mathematical certainty that while hard work and knowledge will get you close, and attitude will get you there, it's the BS that will put you over the top. ~ Author Unknown

64

The Definition of Life

On Nov. 18, 1995, Itzhak Perlman, the violinist, came on stage to give a concert at Avery Fisher Hall at the Lincoln Center in New York City.

If you have ever been to a Perlman concert, you know that getting on stage is no small achievement for him. He was stricken with polio as a child, and so he has braces on both legs and walks with the aid of two crutches. To see him walk across the stage one step at a time, painfully and slowly, is an awesome sight.

He walks painfully, yet majestically, until he reaches his chair. Then he sits down slowly, puts his crutches on the floor, undoes the clasps on his legs, tucks one foot back and extends the other foot forward. Then he bends down and picks up his violin, puts it under his chin, nods to the conductor and proceeds to play.

His fans in the audience and used to his ritual. They sit quietly while he makes his way across the stage to his chair. They remain reverently silent while he undoes the clasps on his legs. They wait patiently.

But this time, something went wrong. Just as he finished the first few bars, one of the strings on his violin broke. You could hear it snap – it went off like gunfire across the room. There was no mistaking what that sound meant and what Perlman had to do.

We figured he would have to get up, put on the clasps again, pick up the crutches and limp his way off stage – to either find another violin or else find another string for this one. But he didn't. Instead, he waited a moment, closed his eyes, set his violin under his chin, and signaled to the conductor to begin.

The orchestra began, and he played from where he had left off with such passion and such power and purity as they had never heard before.

Of course, it is impossible to play a symphonic work with just three strings but that night Itzhak Perman refused to know that widely accepted concept.

You could see him modulating, changing and re-composing the piece in his head. At one point, it sounded like he was re-tuning the strings to get new sounds from them that they had never made before.

When he finished, there was an awesome silence in the room. Then people rose and cheered. Perlman smiled, wiped his brow and raised his bow to quiet us. He spoke, not boastfully, but quietly in a pensive tone, "You know, sometimes it's the artist's task to find out how much music you can still make with what you have left."

These powerful words have stayed in my mind ever since I heard them. And who knows? Perhaps that is the definition of life – not just for artists but for all of us.

The music he made with three stings that night was more beautiful, more sacred and more memorable than any that he had ever made before. Lesson: make music, at first with all that we have, and then, when that is no longer possible, make music with what we have left. ~ Author Unknown

65

Friends are God's Way of Taking Care of Us

I was driving home from a meeting about 5 p.m. one evening and was stuck in traffic on Colorado Blvd. when my car started to choke, sputter and die. I barely managed to coast into a gas station, glad only that I would not be blocking traffic and that would have a somewhat warm spot to wait for the tow truck. The car's engine wouldn't even turn over.

Before I could even make the call, I saw a woman walking out of the quickie mart building. She was suddenly on the ground. It looked like she may have slipped on some ice and fallen by a gas pump, so I got out to see if she was okay.

When I got there, it looked more like she had been overcome by sobs than that she had fallen. She was a young woman but looked really haggard with dark circles under her eyes. She dropped something as I helped her up, and I picked it up to give back to her. It was a nickel.

At that moment, everything came into focus for me: the crying woman, her ancient Suburban crammed full of stuff with three kids in the back seat (one in a car seat), and the gas pump reading $4.95.

I asked her if she was okay and if she needed help. She just kept saying "I don't want my kids to see me crying," so we stood on the other side of the pump from her car.

She said she was driving to California and that things were very hard for her right now.

So I asked, "And you were praying?" That made her back away from me a little, but I assured her I was not a crazy person and said, "He heard you, and He sent me."

I took out my card and swiped it through the card reader on the pump so she could fill up her car completely and, while it was fueling, walked to the McDonald's next door and bought two big bags of food, some gift certificates for more and a big cup of coffee. She gave the food to the kids in the car, who attacked it like wolves, and we stood by the pump eating fries and talking a little.

She told me her name and that she lived in Kansas City. Her boyfriend left two months ago and she had not been able to make ends meet. She knew she wouldn't have money to pay rent January 1st, and finally in desperation called her parents with whom she had not spoken in about five years. They lived in California and said she could come live with them until she got on her feet.

So she packed up everything she owned in the car. She told the kids they were going to California for Christmas, but not that they were going to live there.

I gave her my gloves, a little hug and said a quick prayer with her for safety on the road. As I was walking over to my car, she said, "So, are you like an angel or something?"

This definitely made me cry. I said, "Dear, at this time of year angels are really busy, so sometime God uses regular people."

It was so incredible to be a part of someone else's miracle. And of course, you guessed it, when I got in my car it started right away and got me home without a problem. I'll put it in the shop tomorrow to check, but I suspect the mechanic won't find anything wrong.

Sometimes the angels fly close enough to you that you can hear the flutter of their wings. ~ Author Unknown

66

What Goes Around
Comes Around

One day a man saw an old lady stranded on the side of the road and even in the dim light of the day, he could see she needed help. So he pulled up in front of her Mercedes and got out. His Pontiac was still sputtering when he approached her. Even with the smile on his face, she was worried. No one had stopped to help for the last hour or so. Was he going to hurt her? He didn't look safe; he looked poor and hungry.

He could see that she was frightened, standing out there in the cold. He knew how she felt. It was those chills which only fear can put in you. He said, "I'm here to help you, ma'am. Why don't you wait in the car where it's warm? By the way, my name is Bryan Anderson."

Well, all she had was a flat tire, but for an old lady, that was bad enough. Bryan crawled under the car looking for a place to put the jack, skinning his knuckles a time or two. Soon he was able to change the tire. But he had to get dirty and his hands hurt. As he was tightening up the lug nuts, she rolled down the window and began to talk to him. She told him that she was from St. Louis and was only just passing through. She couldn't thank him enough for coming to her aid.

Bryan just smiled as he closed her trunk. The lady asked how much she owed him. Any amount would have been all right with her. She already imagined all the awful things that could have happened had he not stopped. Bryan never thought twice about being paid, this was not a job to him. This was helping someone in need, and God knows there were plenty who had given him a hand in the past. He had lived his whole life that way, and it never occurred to him to act any other way.

He told her that if she really wanted to pay him back, the next time she saw someone who needed help, she could give that person the assistance they needed, and Bryan added, "And think of me."

He waited until she started her car and drove off. It had been a cold and depressing day but he felt good as he headed for home, disappearing into the twilight.

A few miles down the road the lady saw a small café. She went in to grab a bite to eat, and take the chill off before she made the last leg of her trip home. It was a dingy looking restaurant. Outside were two old gas pumps. The whole scene was unfamiliar to her. The waitress came over and brought a clean towel to wipe her wet hair. She had a sweet smile, one that even being on her feet for the whole day couldn't erase. The lady noticed the waitress was nearly eight months pregnant, but she never let the strain and aches change her attitude. The old lady wondered how someone who had so little could be so giving to a stranger. Then she remembered Bryan.

After the lady finished her meal, she paid with a hundred dollar bill. The waitress quickly went to get change for her hundred dollar bill, but the old lady had slipped right out the door. She was gone by the time the waitress came back. The waitress wondered where the lady could be. Then she noticed something written on the napkin. There were tears in her eyes when she read what the lady wrote:

"You don't owe me anything. I have been there too. Somebody once helped me out, the way I'm helping you. If you really want to pay me back, here is what you do: Do not let this chain of love end with you." Under the napkin were four more $100 bills.

Well, there were tables to clear, sugar bowls to fill and people to serve, but the waitress made it through another day. That night when she got home from work and climbed into bed, she was thinking about the money and what the lady had written. How could the lady have known how much she and her husband needed it? With the baby due next month, it was going to be hard.

She knew how worried her husband was, and as he lay sleeping next to her, she gave him a soft kiss and whispered soft and low, "Everything is going to be all right. I love you, Bryan Anderson."

There is an old saying "What goes around comes around." Let this light shine forever. ~ Author Unknown but this tie-in has a lot of the same words used in a Clay Walker Country song.

67

The Interview with God

I dreamed I had an interview with God.

"So you would like to interview me?" God asked.

"If you have the time," I said.

God smiled. "My time is eternity. What questions do you have in mind for me?"

"What surprises you most about humankind?"

God answered . . .

"That they get bored with childhood, they rush to grow up, and then long to be children again."

"That they lose their health to make money, and then lose their money to restore their health."

"That by thinking anxiously about the future, they forget the present, such that they live in neither the present nor the future."

"That they live as if they will never die, and die as though they had never lived."

God's hand took mine and we were silent for a while.

And then I asked . . .

"As a parent, what are some of life's lessons You want your children to learn?"

"To learn they cannot make anyone love them. All they can do is let themselves be loved."

"To learn to forgive by practicing forgiveness."

"To learn that it only takes a few seconds to open profound wounds in those they love, and it can take many years to heal them."

"To learn that a rich person is not one who has the most, but is one who needs the least."

"To learn that there are people who love them dearly, but simply have not yet learned how to express or show their feelings."

"To learn that two people can look at the same thing and see it differently."

"To learn that it is not enough that they forgive one another, but they must also forgive themselves."

"Thank You for your time," I said humbly.

"Is there anything else you would like your children to know?"

God smiled and said, "Just know that I am here . . . always." ~ Author Unknown

68

The Cracks and Flaws
of Our Life

An elderly Chinese woman had two large pots, each hung on the ends of a pole which she carried across her neck. One of the pots had a crack in it while the other pot was perfect and always delivered a full portion of water. At the end of the long walks from the stream to the house, the cracked pot arrived only half full. For a full two years this went on daily, with the woman bringing home only one and a half pots of water.

Of course, the perfect pot was proud of its accomplishments. But the poor cracked pot was ashamed of its own imperfection, and miserable that it could only do half of what it had been made to do.

After two years of what it perceived to be bitter failure, it spoke to the woman one day by the stream.

"I am ashamed of myself, because this crack in my side causes water to leak out all the way back to your house."

The old woman smiled, "did you notice that there are flowers on your side of the path, but not on the other pot's side? That's because I have always known about your crack so I planted flower seeds on your side of the path and every day while we walk back, you water them. For two years I have been able to pick these beautiful flowers to decorate the table. Without you being just the way you are, there would not be this beauty to grace the house."

Each of us has our own unique flaws. But it's the cracks and flaws we each have that make our lives together so very interesting and rewarding.

You've just got to take each person for what they are and look for the good in them. ~ Author Unknown

69

The Hunting Story

R obert L. Humphrey, an Iwo Jima Marine rifle platoon commander who worked for the State Department during the Cold War, was tasked with resolving a conflict between the U.S. and an allied country in Asia Minor. The local people wanted the Americans to go home, while the Americans had a strategic interest in keeping a missile base open and operational. Humphrey discovered that many of the U.S. servicemen considered the locals "stupid, dumb, dirty, dishonest, untrustworthy, disloyal, cowardly, lazy, unsanitary, immoral, cruel, crazy and downright subhuman."

Understandably, the local people's perception was that the Americans did not view them as equal human beings. Their opposition to the presence of the U.S. installation was based on the fact that they simply wanted to be treated with respect and dignity.

One day, as a diversion from his job, Humphrey decided to go hunting for wild boar with some personnel from the American embassy. They took a truck from the motor pool and headed out to the boondocks, stopping at a village to hire some local men for a few bucks to beat the brush and act as guides. This village was very poor. The huts were made of mud and there was no electricity or running water. The streets were unpaved dirt and the whole village smelled sheep manure. The men looked surly and wore dirty clothes. The women covered their faces and wore pantaloons. Most of the children had runny noses, were barefoot and were dressed in rags.

One American in the truck said, "This place stinks." Another said, "These people live just like animals." Finally, a young Air Force man said, "Yeah, they got nothin' to live for; they may as well be dead."

Then, an old sergeant spoke up from the backseat of the truck. He was the quiet type who never said much. In fact, except for his uniform, he didn't look too different from some of the tough men in the village. He turned to the young airman and said, "You think they got nothin' to live for, do you? Well, if you are so sure, why don't you just take my knife, jump down off the back of this truck, and go try to kill one of them?" Suddenly, there was dead silence in the truck.

Humphrey was amazed. It was the first time that anyone had said anything that had silenced the negative talk about the local people. The sergeant went on to say, "I don't know either why they value their lives so much. Maybe it's those snotty nosed kid, or the women in the pantaloons, but whatever it is, they care about their lives and the lives of their loved ones, same as we Americans do. And if we don't stop talking bad about them, they will kick us out of this country!"

Humphrey asked him what we Americans, with all our wealth, could do to prove our belief in the peasants' equality despite their destitution. The sergeant answered, "You got to be brave enough to jump off the back of this truck, knee deep in the mud and sheep dung. You got to have the courage to walk through this village with a smile on your face. And when you see the smelliest, scariest looking peasant, you got to be able to look him in the face and let him know, just with your eyes, that you know he is a man who hurts like you do, and hopes like you do, and wants for his kids just like we all do." That's what human equality really means. ~ Robert L. Humphrey

70

Emergency Telephone Numbers

When . . .
You're are sad, phone John 14.
You have sinned, phone Psalm 51.
You are facing danger, phone Psalm 91.
People have failed you, phone Psalm 27.
It feels as though God is far from you, phone Psalm 139.
Your faith needs stimulation, phone Hebrews 11.
You are alone and scared, phone Psalm 23.
You are worries, phone Matthew 8:19-34.
You are hurt and critical, phone 1 Corinthians 13.
You wonder about Christianity, phone 2 Corinthians 5:15-18.
You need Christ like insurance, phone Romans 8:1-30.
You are leaving home for a trip, phone Psalm 121.
You are praying for yourself, phone Psalm 87.
You require courage for a task, phone, Joshua 1.
You are depressive, phone, Psalm 27.
You lose faith in mankind, phone Corinthians 13.
It looks like people are unfriendly, phone, John 15.
You are losing hope, phone Psalm 126.
Dealing with fear, phone Psalm 3:47.
You need security, phone Psalm 121:3.
You need assurance, phone Mark 8:35.
When you need reassurance, phone Psalm 145:18.
~ Author Unknown

71

F16 Versus C130

A C-130 aircraft was lumbering along when a cocky F-16 fighter jet flashed by. The jet jockey decided to show off.

The fighter jock told the C-130 pilot, "watch this!" and promptly went into a barrel roll followed by a steep climb. Then he finished with a sonic boom as he broke the sound barrier.

The F-16 pilot asked the C-130 pilot what he thought of that.

The C-130 pilot said, "that was impressive, but watch this!"

The C-130 droned along for about five minutes and then the C-130 pilot came back on and said, "What did you think of that?"

Puzzled, the F-16 pilot asked, "What the heck did you do?" The C-130 pilot chuckled. "I stood up, stretched my legs, walked to the back, went to the bathroom, and got a cup of coffee and a cinnamon roll."

The moral of the story is:

When you are young and foolish, speed and flash may seem like good things.

When you get older and smarter, comfort and dull are not such bad things.

We older folks understand this stuff. ~ Author Unknown

Some of us think we deserve respect simply because of our position. No. Respect must be earned daily. ~ Author Unknown

72

Miracles

A little girl went to her bedroom and pulled a glass jelly jar from its hiding place in the closet. She poured the change out on the floor and counted it carefully. Three times, even. The total had to be exactly perfect. No chance here for mistakes. Carefully placing the coins back in the jar and twisting on the cap, she slipped out the back door and made her way six blocks to Rexall's Drug Store with the big red Indian Chief sign above the door.

She waited patiently for the pharmacist to give her some attention, but he was too busy at the moment. Tess twisted her feet to make a scuffing noise. Nothing. She cleared her throat with the most disgusting sound she could muster. No good. Finally she took a quarter from her jar and banged it on the glass counter. That did it!

"And what do you want?" The pharmacist asked in an annoyed tone of voice. "I'm talking to my brother from Chicago whom I haven't seen in ages," he said without waiting for a reply to his question.

"Well, I want to talk to you about my brother," Tess answered back in the same annoyed tone. "He's really sick and I want to buy a miracle."

"I beg your pardon?" said the pharmacist.

"His name is Andrew and he has something bad growing inside his head and my Daddy says only a miracle can save him now. So how much does a miracle cost?"

"'We don't sell miracles here, little girl. I'm sorry but I can't help you," the pharmacist said, softening a little.

"Listen, I have the money to pay for it," she pressed. "If it isn't enough, I will get the rest. Just tell me how much it costs."

The pharmacist's brother was a well-dressed man who witnessed the entire discussion. He stooped down and asked the little girl, "What kind of a miracle does your brother need?"

"I don't know," Tess replied with her eyes welling up. "I just know he's really sick and Mommy says he needs an operation. But my Daddy can't pay for it, so I want to use my money."

"How much do you have?" asked the man from Chicago.

"One dollar and eleven cents," Tess answered barely audible. "And it's all the money I have, but I can get some more if I need to."

"Well, what a coincidence," smiled the man. "A dollar and eleven cents – the exact price of a miracle for little brothers."

He took her money in one hand and with the other hand he grasped her mitten and said, "Take me to where you live. I want to see your brother and meet your parents. Let's see if I have the miracle you need." That well-dressed man was Dr. Carlton Armstrong, a surgeon who specialized in neuro-surgery.

The operation was completed free of charge and it wasn't long until Andrew was home again and doing well. Mom and Dad were happily talking about the chain of events that had led them to this place.

"That surgery," her Mom whispered, "was a real miracle. I wonder how much it would have cost."

Tess smiled. She knew exactly how much a miracle cost, one dollar and eleven cents, plus the faith of a little child. ~ Author Unknown

In our lives, we never know how many miracles we will need. A miracle is not the suspension of natural law, but the operation of a higher law. ~ Author Unknown

What's Holding You?

A story is told of how in a certain remote part of Africa, hunters anchor a coconut to a tree and drill a hole in it just large enough for a monkey to stick his hand into, but only as long as the hand is open and extended. However, if the monkey makes a fist, his hand will not fit through the hole.

Then a shiny stone is placed in the coconut, big enough to ensure the monkey's hand cannot come out while clinching the stone. The monkey is curious. He is attracted to the shiny object he spots inside the hole. When he sticks in his hand and grasps the shiny, worthless pebble he cannot retrieve it because his hand won't come out.

The monkey is possessive. He won't let go. When the hunters come, the monkey is screaming in fear, but he is captured because he is unwilling to release a shiny, worthless pebble which becomes more important to him than his freedom. ~ Author Unknown

What are you holding onto so tightly that keeps you from getting free? ~ Author Unknown

What is Love?

A group of professional people posed this question to a group of 4 to 8-year-olds, "What does love mean?"

The answers they got were broader and deeper than anyone could have imagined. See what you think:

"When my grandmother got arthritis, she couldn't bend over and paint her toenails anymore. So my grandfather does it for her all the time, even when his hands got arthritis too. That's love." Rebecca - age eight

"When someone loves you, the way they say your name is different. You know that your name is safe in their mouth." Billy - age four

"Love is when a girl puts on perfume and a boy puts on shaving cologne and they go out and smell each other." Karl - age five

"Love is when you go out to eat and give somebody most of your French fries without making them give you any of theirs." Chrissy - age six

"Love is what makes you smile when you're tired." Terri - age four

"Love is when my mommy makes coffee for my daddy and she takes a sip before giving it to him, to make sure the taste is OK." Danny - age seven

"Love is when you kiss all the time. Then when you get tired of kissing, you still want to be together and you talk more. My mommy and daddy are like that. They look gross when they kiss." Emily - age eight

"Love is what's in the room with you at Christmas if you stop opening presents and listen," Bobby - age five

"If you want to learn to love better, you should start with a friend who you hate," Nikka - age six

"There are two kinds of love. Our love. God's love. But God makes both kinds of them." Jenny - age four

"Love is when you tell a guy you like his shirt, then he wears it every day," Noelle - age seven

"Love is like a little old woman and a little old man who are still friends even after they know each other so well." Tommy - age six

"During my piano recital, I was on a stage and scared. I looked at all the people watching me and saw my daddy waving and smiling. He was the only one doing that. I wasn't scared anymore." Cindy - age eight

"My mommy loves me more than anybody. You don't see anyone else kissing me to sleep at night." Clare - Age five

"Love is when mommy gives daddy the best piece of chicken." Elaine -age five

"Love is when mommy sees daddy smelly and sweaty and still says he is handsomer than Robert Redford." Chris - age eight

"Love is when your puppy licks your face even after you left him alone all day." Mary Ann - age four

"I know my older sister loves me because she gives me all her old clothes and has to go out and buy new ones." Lauren - age four

"I let my big sister pick on me because my Mom says she only picks on me because she loves me. So I pick on my baby sister because I love her." Bethany - age four

"When you love somebody, your eyelashes go up and down and little stars come out of you." Karen - age seven

"Love is when mommy sees daddy on the toilet and she doesn't think it's gross." Mark - age six

"You really shouldn't say 'I love you' unless you mean it. But if you mean it, you should say it a lot. People forget." Jessica - age eight

Do YOU know what love is......Prove it to someone today. ~ Author Unknown

Who are You Following?

There was a woman driving through a snowstorm just outside Denver. She was completely lost and struggling under the hazardous weather conditions. She was relieved when she happened upon a snowplow.

Since she was lost, she decided to follow the truck and kept as close to the machine as she could while it removed snow from the road.

At times the blowing snow almost cut off her view, but she kept following. After some time, the snowplow stopped and the driver got out and came back to her car. "Lady, where are you going?" he asked.

"I'm on my way to Denver." she replied.

The truck driver replied, "Well, you'll never get there following me! I'm plowing a parking lot!"

WHO are you following? ~ Author Unknown

76

Blending In

A young police cadet was taking his final exam for the police academy and he read the following question in the exam:

You are on patrol in the outer city when an explosion occurs in a gas main in a nearby street. On investigation you find that a large hole has been blown in the road and there is an overturned van nearby. Inside the van there is a strong smell of alcohol. Both occupants – a man and a woman-are injured. You recognize the woman as the wife of your chief of police, who is at currently out of the country.

A passing motorist stops to offer you assistance, and you realize he is wanted for armed robbery. Suddenly a man runs out of a nearby house, shouting that his wife is expecting a baby and the shock of the explosion has made the birth imminent. Another man is crying for help, having been blown into the adjacent canal by the explosion, and he cannot swim.

Describe in a few words what actions you would take.

The young man thought for a moment, picked up his pen and wrote, "I would take off my uniform and mingle with the crowd."

In overwhelming times, we may be tempted to view our responsibility as leaders in life in much the same way.

Don't blend in....LEAD THE WAY! ~ Author Unknown

Five Best Sayings to Remember (5-4-3-2-1)

There's a simple way to summarize how to be your best in five simple sayings using the English language.

Five favorite words in the English language: *God Created All Men Equal.* Equality is not understood all over the world; it is everyone's job and duty to go forth and do their very best to change this.

Four favorite words in the English language: *Live a Balanced Life.* Live a balanced life where you spend as much time mentally, emotionally, physically and spiritually honing yourself to be a mentor of others. You need these wonderful traits to live that balanced life.

Three favorite words in the English language: *I Love You.* There is no love like unconditional love. Love all your fellow service members, family and friends. Love them with their strengths and weaknesses. Love them as you would want to be loved.

Two favorite words in the English language: *Genuine Concern.* Take care of others before taking care of yourself. Be there for your family, friends and others 24/7/365.

One favorite word in the English language: *Humility.* It's not about you. Be humble. You know your accomplishments in life and so does God. No one else

really needs to know. ~ MajGen Thomas Jones, U.S. Marine
Retired

78

Warrior's Creed

Wherever I go, everyone is a little safer.
Wherever I am, anyone in need has a friend.
When I return home, everyone is happy I am there.

It's a better life!

~ Robert L. Humphrey

79

Words To Ponder

If we ever forget that we're one nation under God, then we will be a nation gone under. ~ Ronald Reagan

All achievements, all earned riches, have their beginning in an idea. ~ Napoleon Hill

The significant problems we face cannot be solved at the same level of thinking we were at when we created them. ~ Albert Einstein

Most folks are as happy as they make up their minds to be. ~ Abraham Lincoln

80

Your Weakness

This is the story of a 10-year-old boy who decided to study judo despite the fact he had lost his left arm in a devastating car accident. The boy began lessons with an old Japanese judo master. The boy was doing well, so he couldn't understand why, after three months of training, the master had taught him only one move. "Sensei," the boy finally said, "Shouldn't I be learning more moves?"

"This is the only move you know, but this is the only move you'll ever need to know," the Sensei replied. Not quite understanding, but believing in his teacher, the boy kept training.

Several months later, the Sensei took the boy to his first tournament. Surprising himself, the boy easily won his first two matches. The third match proved to be more difficult, but after some time, his opponent became impatient and charged; the boy deftly used his one move to win the match. Still amazed by his success, the boy was now in the finals.

This time, his opponent was bigger, stronger and more experienced. For a while, the boy appeared to be overmatched. Concerned that the boy might get hurt, the referee called a time-out. He was about to stop the match when the Sensei intervened. "No," the Sensei insisted, "Let him continue."

Soon after the match resumed, his opponent made a critical mistake: he dropped his guard. Instantly, the boy used his move to pin him. The boy won the match and the tournament. He was the champion.

On the way home, the boy and Sensei reviewed every move in each and every match. Then the boy summoned the courage to ask what was really on his mind. "Sensei, how did I win the tournament with only one move?"

"You won for two reasons," the Sensei answered. "First, you've almost mastered one of the most difficult throws in all of judo. And second, the only known defense for that move is for your opponent to grab your left arm."

The boy's greatest weakness had become his greatest strength. ~ Author Unknown

If a man does his best, what else is there? ~ General George S. Patton

I find that the harder I work the more luck I seem to have. ~ Thomas Jefferson

Patience is the companion of wisdom. ~ Saint Augustine

81

May This Encourage You, Always

If there are people in your life who continually disappoint you, break promises, stomp on your dreams, are too judgmental, have different values and don't have your back during difficult times: that is not friendship.

To have a friend, be a friend. Sometimes in life as you grow, your friends will either grow or go. Surround yourself with people who reflect your values, goals, interests and lifestyles.

When I think of any of my successes, I am thankful to God from whom all blessings flow, and to my family and friends who enrich my life.

Over the years my phone book has changed because I changed, for the better. At first, you think you're going to be alone, but after a while, new people show up in your life who make it so much sweeter and easier to endure.

Remember what your elders used to say, "Birds of a feather flock together. If you're an eagle, don't hang around chickens: Chickens can't fly!" ~ Author Unknown

82

Your Keepers

I grew up in the fifties with practical parents including a mother, God love her, who washed aluminum foil after she cooked in it, then reused it. She was the original recycle queen, before they had a name for it. My father who was happier getting old shoes fixed than buying new ones.

Their marriage was good, their dreams focused. Their best friends lived barely a wave away. I can see them now, dad in trousers, tee shirt and a hat, and mom in a housedress.

It was the time for fixing things – a curtain rod, the kitchen radio, screen door, the oven door, and the hem in a dress. Things we keep. It was a way of life, and sometimes it made me crazy. All that fixing, reheating, renewing, I wanted just once to be wasteful; waste meant affluence. Throwing things away meant you knew there'd always be more.

But then my mother died, and on that clear summer's night, in the warmth of the hospital room, I was struck with the pain of learning that sometimes there isn't any more. Sometimes, what we care about most goes away... never to return. So, while we have it, it's best we love it and care for it; fix it when it's broken, and heal it when it's sick. This is true for marriage, old radios, old cars, children with bad report cards, dogs with bad hips, aging parents and grandparents.

There are just some things that make life important: like people we know who are special, so keep them close. Who are the keepers in your life? ~ Author Unknown

83

Illuminated by Blindness

There was a blind girl who hated herself because she was blind. She hated everyone, except her loving boyfriend. He was always there for her. She told her boyfriend, "If I could only see the world, I would marry you."

One day, someone donated a pair of eyes to her. When the bandages came off, she was able to see everything including her boyfriend.

He asked her, "Now that you can see the world, will you marry me?" The girl looked at her boyfriend and saw that he was blind. The sight of his closed eyelids shocked her. She hadn't expected that. The thought of looking at them the rest of her life led her to refuse to marry him.

Her boyfriend left in tears and days later had a note sent to her saying, "Take good care of your eyes, my dear, for before they were yours they were mine."

This is often how our human nature works when our status changes. Only a very few remember what life was like before, and who was always by their side in the most painful situations.

Life is a gift. Today, before you say an unkind word, think of someone who can't speak. Before you complain about the taste of your food, think of someone who has nothing to eat.

Before you complain about your husband or wife, think of someone who's crying out to God for a companion.

Today, before you complain about life, think of those who may have died before their time.

Before whining about the distance you drive, think of those who walk the same distance on foot.

When you are tired and complain about your job, think of the unemployed, the disabled and those who wish they had your job.

And, when depressing thoughts seem to get you down, put a smile on your face and think: you're alive and still around for a reason. ~ Author Unknown

84

Two Brothers

Once upon a time two brothers, who lived on adjoining farms, fell into conflict. It was the first serious rift in 40 years of farming side by side, sharing machinery, and trading labor and goods as needed without disagreement. Then the long collaboration fell apart. It began with a small misunderstanding and it grew into a major difference. Finally it exploded into an exchange of bitter words followed by weeks of silence.

One morning there was a knock on John's door. He opened it to find a man with a carpenter's tool box. "I'm looking for a few days' work," he said. "Perhaps you would have a few small jobs here and there I could help with? Could I help you?"

"Yes," said the older brother. "I do have a job for you."

"Look across the creek at that farm. That's my neighbor; in fact, he's my younger brother. Last week there was a meadow between us and he took his bulldozer to the river levee and now there is a creek between us. Well, he may have done this to spite me, but I'll do him one better."

"See that pile of lumber by the barn? I want you to build me an eight-foot fence so I won't have to see his place or his face anymore."

The carpenter said, "I think I understand the situation. Show me the nails and the post-hole digger and I'll be able to do a job that pleases you."

The older brother had to go to town, so he helped the carpenter get the materials ready and then he was off for the day. The carpenter worked hard all that day measuring, sawing and nailing. About sunset when the farmer returned, the carpenter had just finished his job.

The farmer's eyes opened wide, his jaw dropped. There was no fence there at all. It was a bridge, a bridge stretching from one side of the creek to the other! A fine piece of work, handrails and all, and the neighbor, his younger brother, was coming toward them, his hand outstretched.

"You are quite a fellow to build this bridge after all I've said and done." The two brothers stood at each end of the bridge, and then they met in the middle, taking each other's hand.

They turned to see the carpenter hoist his toolbox onto his shoulder. "No, wait! Stay a few days, please. I've a lot of other projects for you," said the older brother. "I'd love to stay on," the carpenter said, "but I have many more bridges to build. ~ Author Unknown

They say it takes a minute to find a special person, an hour to appreciate them, a day to love them, but then an entire life to forget them. Keep in touch with your friends; you never know when you'll need each other. ~ Author Unknown

85

Rain

She had been shopping with her Mom at Wal-Mart. She must have been about 6-years old. She was a beautiful red-haired, freckle faced image of innocence. It was pouring outside. It was the kind of rain that gushes over the top of rain gutters, so much in a hurry to hit the earth it has no time to flow down the spout. We all stood there under the awning and just inside the door of the Wal-Mart. We waited, some patiently, others irritated because nature messed up their hurried day.

I am always mesmerized by rainfall. I got lost in the sound and sight of the heavens washing away the dirt and dust of the world. Memories were a welcome reprieve from the worries of my day.

Her voice was so sweet as it broke the hypnotic trance we were all caught in, "Mom, let's run through the rain," she said.

"What?" Mom asked.

"Let's run through the rain!" She repeated.

"No, honey. We'll wait until it slows down a bit," Mom replied.

This young child waited about another minute and repeated: "Mom, let's run through the rain."

"We'll get soaked if we do," Mom said.

"No, we won't, Mom. That's not what you said this morning," the young girl said as she tugged at her Mom's arm.

"This morning? When did I say we could run through the rain and not get wet?"

"Don't you remember? When you were talking to Daddy about his cancer, you said, 'If God can get us through this, he can get us through anything!'"

The entire crowd stopped dead silent. I swear you couldn't hear anything but the rain. We all stood silently. No one came or left for a few long minutes.

Mom paused and thought for a moment about what she would say. Now some would laugh it off and scold her for being silly. Some might even ignore what was said. But this was a moment of affirmation in a young child's life. A time when innocent trust can be nurtured so that it will bloom into faith.

"Honey, you are absolutely right. Let's run through the rain. If GOD lets us get wet, well maybe we just needed washing," Mom said. Then off they ran.

We all stood watching, smiling and laughing as they darted past the cars and yes, through the puddles. They held their shopping bags over their heads just in case. They got soaked. They were followed by a few who screamed and laughed like children all the way to their cars. And yes, I did. I ran. I got wet. I needed washing.

Circumstances or people can take away your material possessions, they can take away your money, and they can take away your health. But no one can ever take away your precious memories. So, don't forget to make time and take the opportunities to make memories every day.

"To everything there is a season and a time to every purpose under heaven." ~ Author Unknown

I HOPE YOU STILL TAKE THE TIME TO RUN THROUGH THE RAIN.

86

What are You Looking to Feast Upon?

Both the hummingbird and the vulture fly over our country's lands.

All vultures see is rotting meat, because that is what they seek. They thrive on that diet.

But hummingbirds ignore the smelly flesh of dead animals. Instead, they look for the colorful blossoms of beautiful plants.

The vultures live on what was. They live on the past. They fill themselves with what is dead and gone.

But hummingbirds live on what is. They seek new life. They fill themselves with freshness and life.

Each bird finds what it is looking for. We all do.

What are you looking to feast upon? ~ Author Unknown

Make a decision, communicate that decision and then execute it. Life is not a dress rehearsal! You only have one shot on this earth, make it your best shot! ~ Joe Shusko

87

Lucky

Mary and her husband, Jim, had a dog named Lucky. Lucky was a real character. Whenever Mary and Jim had company come for a weekend visit they would warn their friends not leave their luggage open because Lucky would help himself to whatever struck his fancy. Inevitably, someone would forget and something would come up missing.

Mary or Jim would go to Lucky's toy box in the basement and there the treasure would be, amid all of Lucky's other favorite toys. Lucky always stashed his finds in his toy box and he was very particular that his toys stay in the box.

It happened that Mary found out she had breast cancer. Something told her she was going to die of this disease....in fact; she was just sure it was fatal.

She scheduled the double mastectomy, fear riding her shoulders. The night before she was to go to the hospital she cuddled with Lucky. A thought struck her...what would happen to Lucky? Although the 3-year-old dog liked Jim, he was Mary's dog through and through. If I die, Lucky will feel abandoned, Mary thought. He won't understand that I didn't want to leave him. The thought made her sadder than thinking of her own death.

The double mastectomy was harder on Mary than her doctors had anticipated and Mary was hospitalized for more than two weeks. Jim took Lucky for his evening walk faithfully, but the little dog just drooped, kept whining and seemed miserable.

Finally the day came for Mary to leave the hospital. When she arrived home, Mary was so exhausted she couldn't even make it up the steps to her bedroom. Jim made his wife comfortable on the couch and left her to nap. Lucky stood watching Mary but he didn't come to her when she called. It made Mary sad but sleep soon overcame her and she dozed.

When Mary woke for a second she couldn't understand what was wrong. She couldn't move her head and her body felt heavy and hot. But panic soon gave way to laughter when Mary realized the problem. She was covered, literally blanketed, with every treasure Lucky owned! While she had slept, the sorrowing dog had made trip after trip to the basement bringing his beloved mistress all his favorite things in life. He had covered her with his love.

Mary forgot about dying. Instead she and Lucky began living again, walking further and further together every day.

It's been 12 years now and Mary is still cancer-free. Lucky? He still steals treasures and stashes them in his toy box but Mary remains his greatest treasure.

Remember: live every day to the fullest. Each minute is a blessing from God. And never forget: the people who make a difference in our lives are not the ones with the most credentials, the most money or the most awards, they are the ones who care for us. ~ Author Unknown

88

The Sack Lunches

I put my carry-on in the luggage compartment and sat down in my assigned seat. It was going to be a long flight. "I'm glad I have a good book to read. Perhaps, I will get a short nap," I thought.

Just before take-off, a line of soldiers came down the aisle and filled all the vacant seats, totally surrounding me. I decided to start a conversation.

"Where are you headed?" I asked the soldier seated nearest to me.

"Chicago – to Great Lakes Base. We'll be there for two weeks for special training, and then we're being deployed to Iraq."

After flying for about an hour, an announcement was made that sack lunches were available for five dollars. It would be several hours before we reached Chicago, and I quickly decided a lunch would help pass the time. As I reached for my wallet, I overheard soldier ask his buddy if he planned to buy lunch. "No, that seems like a lot of money for just a sack lunch. Probably wouldn't be worth five bucks. I'll wait till we get to Chicago." His friend agreed.

I looked around at the other soldiers. None were buying lunch. I walked to the back of the plane and handed the flight attendant a fifty dollar bill. "Take a lunch to all those soldiers."

She grabbed my arms and squeezed tightly. Her eyes wet with tears, she thanked me. "My son was a soldier in Iraq; it's almost like you are doing it for him."

Picking up ten sacks, she headed up the aisle to where the soldiers were seated. She stopped at my seat and asked, "Which do you like best – beef or chicken?"

"Chicken," I replied, wondering why she asked.

She turned and went to the front of plane, returning a minute later with a dinner plate from first class. "This is your thanks."

After we finished eating, I went again to the back of the plane, heading for the rest room. A man stopped me.

"I saw what you did. I want to be part of it. Here, take this." He handed me twenty-five dollars.

Soon after I returned to my seat, I saw the Flight Captain coming down the aisle, looking at the aisle numbers as he walked, I hoped he was not looking for me, but noticed he was looking at the numbers only on my side of the plane. When he got to my row he stopped, smiled, held out his hand, and said, "I want to shake your hand."

Quickly unfastening my seatbelt I stood and took the Captain's hand. With a booming voice he said, "I was a soldier and I was a military pilot. Once, someone bought me a lunch. It was an act of kindness I never forgot."

I was embarrassed when applause was heard from all of the passengers.

Later I walked to the front of the plane so I could stretch my legs. A man who was seated about six rows in front of me reached out his hand, wanting to shake mine. He left another twenty-five dollars in my palm.

When we landed in Chicago I gathered my belongings and started to deplane. Waiting just inside the airplane door was a man who stopped me, put something in my shirt pocket, turned, and walked away without saying a word. Another twenty-five dollars!

Upon entering the terminal, I saw the soldiers gathering for their trip to the base. I walked over to them and handed them seventy-five dollars. "It will take you some time to reach the base. It will be about time for a sandwich. God Bless You."

Ten young men left that flight feeling the love and respect of their fellow travelers. As I walked briskly to my car, I whispered a prayer for their safe return. These soldiers were giving their all for our country. I could only give them a couple of meals. It seemed so little.

A veteran is someone who, at one point in his life wrote a blank check made payable to "The United States of America" for an amount of up to and including his or her life. That is Honor, and there are way too many people in this country who no longer understand it. ~ Author Unknown

And so my fellow Americans, ask not what your country can do for you; ask what you can do for your country. ~ John F. Kennedy

89

Stress and a Glass of Water

A lecturer, when explaining stress management to an audience, raised a glass of water and asked, "How heavy is this glass of water?"

Answers called out ranged from 20g to 500g.

The lecturer replied, "The absolute weight doesn't matter. It depends on how long you try to hold it.

If I hold it for a minute, that's not a problem.

If I hold it for an hour, I'll have an ache in my right arm.

If I hold it for a day, you'll have to call an ambulance.

In each case, it's the same weight, but the longer I hold it, the heavier it becomes."

He continued, "And that's the way it is with stress management. If we carry our burdens all the time, sooner or later, as the burden becomes increasingly heavier, we won't be able to carry on."

"As with the glass of water, you have to put it down for a while and rest before holding it again. When we're refreshed, we can carry on with the burden."

"So, before you return home tonight, put the burden of work down. Don't carry it home. You can pick it up tomorrow. Whatever burdens you're carrying now, set them down and don't pick them up again until after you've rested a while. Here are some great ways of dealing with the burdens of life:

- Accept that on some days you're the pigeon, and some days you're the statue.
- Always keep your words soft and sweet, just in case you have to eat them.
- Always read stuff that will make you look good if you die in the middle of it.
- Drive carefully. It's not only cars that can be recalled by their Maker.
- If you can't be kind, at least have the decency to be vague.
- If you lend someone $20 and never see that person again, it was probably worth it.
- It may be that your sole purpose in life is simply to be kind to others.
- Never put both feet in your mouth at the same time, because you won't have a leg to stand on.
- The second mouse gets the cheese.
- When everything's coming your way, you're in the wrong lane.
- Birthdays are good for you. The more you have, the longer you live.
- You may be the only person in the world, but you may also be the world to one person.
- Some mistakes are too much fun to only make once.
- We could learn a lot from crayons. Some are sharp, some are pretty, and some are dull. Some have weird names and all are different colors, but they all have to live in the same box."
- A truly happy person is one who can enjoy the scenery on a detour. ~ Author Unknown

LIVE simply, LOVE/GIVE generously, CARE deeply, SPEAK kindly and LEAVE! ~ Ronald Reagan

90

The Cross

A young man was at the end of his rope, seeing no way out, he dropped to his knees in prayer. "Lord, I can't go on," he said. "I have too heavy a cross to bear."

The Lord replied, "My son, if you can't bear its weight, just place your cross inside this room. Then, open that other door and pick out any cross you wish."

The man was filled with relief and said, "Thank you, Lord," and he did as he was told.

Upon entering the other room, he saw many crosses; some so large the tops were not visible. Then, he spotted a tiny cross leaning against a far wall.

"I'd like that one, Lord," he whispered.

The Lord replied, "My son that is the cross you just brought in."

When life's problems seem overwhelming, it helps to look around and see what other people are coping with. You may consider yourself far more fortunate than you imagine.

Whatever your cross, whatever your pain,
There will always be sunshine after the rain.
Perhaps you may stumble,
Perhaps even fall.
But God's always there,
To help you through it all. ~ Author Unknown

91

Deck of Cards

It was quiet that day. The guns, mortars and land mines, for some reason, hadn't been heard. The young Marine knew it was Sunday, the holiest day of the week.

As he was sitting there, he got out an old deck of cards and laid them out across his bunk.

Just then his sergeant came in and said, "Why aren't you with the rest of the platoon?"

The Marine replied, "I thought I would stay behind and spend some time with the Lord."

The sergeant said, "Looks to me like you're going to play cards."

"No, sir," replied the young man. "You see, since we are not allowed to have Bibles or other spiritual books in this country, I've decided to talk to the Lord by studying this deck of cards."

The sergeant asked in disbelief, "How will you do that?"

"You see the Ace, Sergeant? It reminds me that there is only one God.

The Two represents the two parts of the Bible, Old and New Testaments.

The Three represents the Father, Son and the Holy Ghost.

The Four stands for the Four Gospels: Matthew, Mark, Luke and John.

The Five is for the five virgins – there were ten but only five of them were glorified.

The Six is for the six days it took God to create the Heavens and Earth.

The Seven is for the day God rested after making His Creation.

The Eight is for the family of Noah and his wife, their three sons and their wives – the eight people God spared from the flood that destroyed the Earth.

The Nine is for the lepers whom Jesus cleansed of leprosy. He cleansed ten, but nine never thanked Him.

The Ten represents the Ten Commandments that God handed down to Moses on tablets made of stone.

The Jack is a reminder of Satan, one of God's first angels, who got kicked out of heaven for his wicked ways and is now the joker of eternal hell.

The Queen stands for the Virgin Mary.

The King stands for Jesus, for he is the King of all kings.

When I count the dots on all the cards, I come up with 365 total, one for every day of the year.

There are a total of 52 cards in a deck; each is a week – 52 weeks in a year.

The four suits represent the four seasons: spring, summer, fall and winter.

Each suit has thirteen cards and there are exactly thirteen weeks in a quarter.

So when I want to talk to God and thank Him, I just pull out this old deck of cards and they remind me of all that I have to be thankful for."

The sergeant just stood there. After a minute, with pain in his heart, he said, "Marine, can I borrow that deck of cards?" ~ Author Unknown

92

The Haircut

A teenage boy who had just passed his driving test asked his father if they could discuss his use of the car.

His father said he'd make a deal with his son. "You bring your grades up, study your Bible a little, get your haircut, and then we'll talk about the car."

The boy thought about that for a moment and then agreed to the offer.

After about six weeks his father said, "Son, I'm proud of you. Your school grades have improved and I've noticed that you have been studying your Bible.

My only disappointment is that you haven't had your haircut."

The young man paused a moment then said, "You know, Dad, I've been thinking about that, and I've noticed in my studies of the Bible that Samson had long hair, John the Baptist had long hair, Moses had long hair and there's even a strong argument that Jesus had long hair."

To this his father replied, "Did you also notice they all walked everywhere they went?" ~ Author Unknown

Believe in yourself the way I do, and nothing will be beyond your reach. ~ Author Unknown

A pessimist is one who makes difficulties of his opportunities and an optimist is one who makes opportunities of his difficulties. ~ Harry Truman

93

Life

Here, there are no winners,
And losers only by default,
We speed up to go nowhere,
In search of that which is not sought.

Our hearts are so innocent,
Our minds are feeble and numb,
We look to be the "Good Guy,"
But there are no heroes to go unsung.

We set out to change the world,
Our intentions are as pure as gold,
We allow life to get in the way of living,
And instead of selling, we are sold.

Life is really what we make of it,
And whether we choose to take a stand,
And march to the beat of a different drummer,
Or continue to march with the band.

As we struggle through life and death my friends,
Let us always and forever keep in mind,
That your life only has meaning when shared with others,
Since the fruit always dies when separated from the vine.

We will continue striving to reconcile,
That which we have not paid a price,
Our lives are really not ours to give,
We are bought and paid for by the blood of Christ.

~ Philip A. Wilson

94

Cup of Motivation

There is no time like the present to start the year off right with this first cup of MOTIVATION! Take a big gulp! That said, what is your DREAM?

Congratulations! As Dr. Seuss would say, "Today is your day; you're off to great places. You're off and away!"

What do you want to do this year as a Marine, husband, father, friend? Whose lives are you going to impact TODAY, TOMORROW and the rest of their lives?

What's your ONE MAIN GOAL for yourself?

There's no time to worry or second guess, take the JUMP! Have a PASSION! Be the LEADER!

Stu Weber says, "There are Four Pillars of a Man's Heart!"

"King – look ahead, watch over and provides. Men are the providers!

Warrior – shields, defends, guards and protects. Men stand tallest when they are protecting and defending!

Mentor – teaches, models, explains and trains. Men are supposed to be able to teach life!

Friend – commitment-maker, promise-keeper, one who connects. Men connect pieces together to make someone better!"

Know this! YOU were born for Victory! Why?

Jeremiah 29:11 says, "For I know the plans I have for you" declares the Lord. "Plans to prosper you and not to harm you, plans to give you hope and a future."

"And will you succeed? Yes! You will indeed! (98 3/4 percent guaranteed!) Kid, you'll move MOUNTAINS!" ~ Dr. Seusse

Romans 10:14-15 says, "How can THEY know who to trust if THEY haven't heard of the ONE who can be trusted. And how can THEY hear if nobody tells them. And how is anyone going to TELL THEM, UNLESS SOMEONE is sent to DO IT!"

Don't do something good! Do something GREAT! So go forth and CONQUER! ~ Brian Woodall, USMC

95

Layman's Language 10 Commandments

1. Prayer is not a "spare wheel" that you pull out when in trouble, but it is a "steering wheel" that directs the right path.
2. Why is a car's WINDSHIELD so large and the rear view mirror is so small? Because our PAST is not as important as our FUTURE. So, look ahead and move on.
3. Friendship is like a BOOK. It takes few seconds to burn but it takes years to write.
4. All things in life are temporary. If going well, enjoy it, they will not last forever. If going wrong, don't worry, they don't last forever; joy comes in the morning.
5. Old friends are gold! New friends are diamonds! If you get a diamond, don't forget the gold! Because to hold a diamond, you always need a base of gold!
6. Often when we lose hope and think this is the end, GOD smiles from above and says, "Relax, it's just a bend, not the end!
7. When GOD solves your problems, you have faith in HIS abilities; when GOD doesn't solve your problems, HE has faith in your abilities.

8. A blind person asked St. Anthony, "Can there be anything worse than losing eye sight?" He replied: "Yes, losing your vision!"

9. When you pray for others, God listens to you and blesses them and when you are safe and happy, remember someone has prayed for you.

10. WORRYING does not take away tomorrow's TROUBLES; it takes away today's PEACE. ~ Author Unknown

We trust, sir that God is on our side. It is more important to know that we are on God's side. ~ Abraham Lincoln

96

Man Cuts Hand Off...
For the Second Time!

A meat worker in New Zealand who accidentally cut his hand off with a saw had the operation to reattach it complicated by the fact that he'd previously cut the same arm off in a previous accident.

Bryan Speers almost completely severed his left hand at the wrist while cutting a flap of meat with a band saw at Crusader Meats.

He told the New Zealand Herald, "I just grabbed my hand and walked down to the office swearing my head off. I really thought I was going to die."

Colleagues taped the hand back on and Speers was taken to the hospital in an ambulance. However, surgeons trying to sew the hand back on ran into problems both because of the amount of damage to the limb, and the fact that his arm was still scarred from a previous accident.

Doctor Katerina Anesti of the Waikato Hospital said, "He had nearly cut off the same arm before about five centimeters up his arm. The scarring made it difficult to know what was what."

The operation was eventually successful. However, Speers is expected to remain in the hospital for several more days, and his rehabilitation could take months.

We all make mistakes. That is part of the "Human Condition." We fail, we seek correction, we learn, we move on and we succeed. But if we do not learn from our mistakes, we show a lack of wisdom.

Let us strive to learn from our failures, seek forgiveness, make improvement and move on. ~ Author Unknown

"God is faithful and reliable. If we confess our sins, He forgives them and cleanses us from everything we've done wrong." ~ 1 John 1:9 GOD'S WORD Translation

97

14 Marine Corps Leadership Traits

- **Dependability**: The certainty of proper performance of duty.
- **Bearing**: Creating a favorable impression in carriage, appearance and personal conduct at all times.
- **Courage**: The mental quality that recognizes fear of danger or criticism, but enables a person to proceed in the face of it with calmness and firmness.
- **Decisiveness**: The ability to make decisions promptly and to announce them in clear, forceful manner.
- **Endurance**: The mental and physical stamina measured by the ability to withstand pain, fatigue, stress and hardship.
- **Enthusiasm**: The display of sincere interest and exuberance in the performance of duty.
- **Initiative**: Taking action in the absence of orders.
- **Integrity**: Uprightness of character and soundness of moral principles; includes the qualities of truthfulness and honesty.
- **Judgment**: The ability to weigh facts and possible solutions on which to base sound decisions.
- **Justice**: Giving reward and punishment according to merits of the case in question. The ability to administer a system of rewards and punishments impartially and consistently.

- **Knowledge**: Understanding of a science or an art. The range of one's information, including professional knowledge and an understanding of your Marines.
- **Tact**: The ability to deal with others without creating offense.
- **Unselfishness**: Avoidance of providing for one's own comfort and personal advancement at the expense of others.
- **Loyalty**: The quality of faithfulness to country, the Corps, the unit, to one's seniors, subordinates and peers.

Marine Corps Leadership Principles

- Know yourself and seek self-improvement.
- Be technically and tactically proficient.
- Develop a sense of responsibility among your subordinates.
- Make sound and timely decisions.
- Know your Marines and look out for their welfare.
- Keep your Marines informed.
- Seek responsibility and take responsibility for your actions.
- Train your Marines as a team.
- Employ your command in accordance with its capabilities.
- Ensure assigned tasks are understood, supervised and accomplished.

The Magic of Loving Discipline

When I turned 16, I wanted a car right away! My mom cautioned me to wait and she would help me, but I made a "deal" with a guy I worked with at a fast food restaurant and bought his car that very week.

I didn't check into the quality of the engine and the car did not even have a "clean" title. As a result, I had to deal with a never-ending string of mechanical trouble and paperwork until the day I sold that piece of junk.

Sometimes God's best discipline is giving us exactly what we want.

In many cases, our ability to discern what is best for us is flawed. The things we trust to make us happy often turn out to be painful mistakes that force us to grow and mature.

As parents, it can be tough to allow our kids to make mistakes but lessons from experience are usually the most effective.

Allowing your kids to make mistakes and suffer consequences in a grace-filled environment can be the best form of loving discipline. ~ Author Unknown

The ultimate result of shielding men from the effects of folly is to fill the world with fools. ~ Herbert Spencer (1820 - 1903)

100

Live Life BACKWARDS!

Close your eyes.
Imagine a funeral.
You look around the room and you know those who are in attendance.

Loved ones ....friends.

You realize this is YOUR funeral.

You see the person closest to you in the whole world step to the front and begin to speak.

What do you want them to say?

Now go live in such a way as to make those words true. ~ Author Unknown

There are four ways, and only four ways, in which we have contact with the world. We are evaluated and classified by these four contacts: what we do, how we look, what we say, and how we say it. ~ Dale Carnegie

101

Inner Peace: Think About it!

If you can start the day without caffeine,
If you can always be cheerful, ignoring aches and pains,
If you can resist complaining and boring people with your troubles,
If you can eat the same food every day and be grateful for it,
If you can understand when your loved ones are too busy to give you any time,
If you can take criticism and blame without resentment,
If you can conquer tension without medical help,
If you can relax without alcohol,
If you can sleep without the aid of drugs,
...Then You Are Probably.........The Family Dog!
~ Author Unknown

What is the Price for Your Honor?

Is your honor for sale?

A high ranking bank official approached the newly hired accountant and whispered into his ear, "If I paid you $500,000.00, would you help me 'adjust' the books?"

The young man looked around the room hesitantly and slowly nodded, "yes sir," he whispered.

The bank official shrugged and said, "Would you do it for $5,000.00?"

Offended the accountant stepped back and said, rather harshly, "Sir! What do you think I am, a common thief?"

"We have already established that fact," he replied. "Now we are simply negotiating your price." ~ Author Unknown

For what does it profit a man to gain the whole world, and forfeit his soul? ~ Mark 8:36

103

Making Pancakes

Six-year old Brandon decided one Saturday morning to fix his parents pancakes. He found a big bowl and spoon, pulled a chair to the counter, opened the cupboard and pulled out the heavy flour canister, spilling it on the floor.

He scooped some of the flour into the bowl with his hands, mixed in most of a cup of milk and added some sugar, leaving a floury trail on the floor which by now had a few tracks left by his kitten. Brandon was covered with flour and getting frustrated. He wanted this to be something very good for Mom and Dad, but it was getting very bad.

He didn't know what to do next, whether to put it all into the oven or on the stove and he didn't know how the stove worked! Suddenly, he saw his kitten licking from the bowl of mix, reached to push her away, knocking the egg carton to the floor. Frantically, he tried to clean up this monumental mess but slipped on the eggs, getting his pajamas soiled with flour and sticky with the eggs.

And just then he saw Dad standing at the door. Big crocodile tears welled up in Brandon's eyes. All he'd wanted to do was something good, but he'd made a terrible mess. He was sure a scolding was coming, maybe even a spanking. But his father just watched him.

Then, walking through the mess, he picked up his crying son, hugged him tightly, getting his own pajamas messy and sticky in the process! That's how God deals with us. Sometimes we try to do something good in life, but it turns into a mess.

Our marriage gets all sticky or we insult a friend, or we can't stand our job, or our health goes sour. Sometimes we just stand there in tears because we can't think of anything else to do.

That's when God picks us up and loves us and forgives us, even though some of our mess gets all over Him. But just because we might mess up, we can't stop trying to "make pancakes" for God or for others. Sooner or later we'll get it right, and then they'll be glad we tried.

I was thinking and I wondered if I had any wounds needing to be healed, friendships that need rekindling or three words needing to be said. Sometimes, "I love you" can heal and bless!

Remind every one of your friends that you love them. Even if you think they don't love back, you would be amazed at what those three little words, a smile, and a reminder like this can do.

Just in case I haven't told you lately... I LOVE YA!!! Suppose one morning you were called to God; do all your friends know you love them? ~ Author Unknown

104

You Have to Love German Shepherds

One day an old German Shepherd starts chasing rabbits and before long, discovers he's lost. Wandering about, he notices a panther heading rapidly in his direction with the intention of having the old canine for lunch.

The old German Shepherd thinks, "Oh, oh! I'm in deep trouble now!"

Noticing some bones on the ground close by, he immediately settles down to chew on the bones with his back to the approaching cat. Just as the panther is about to leap, the old German Shepherd exclaims loudly,

"Boy that was one delicious panther! I wonder if there are any more around here?"

Hearing this, the young panther halts his attack in mid-strike, a look of terror comes over him and he slinks away into the trees.

"Whew!" says the panther, "That was close! That old German Shepherd nearly had me!"

Meanwhile, a squirrel who had been watching the whole scene from a nearby tree, figures he can put this knowledge to good use and trade it for protection from the panther. So, off he goes.

The squirrel soon catches up with the panther, spills the beans and strikes a deal for himself with the panther.

The young panther is furious at being made a fool and says, "Here, squirrel, hop on my back and see what's going to happen to that conniving canine!"

Now, the old German Shepherd sees the panther coming with the squirrel on his back and thinks, "What am I going to do now?" But instead of running, the dog sits down with his back to his attackers, pretending he hasn't seen them yet, and just when they get close enough to hear, the old German Shepherd says,

"Where's that squirrel? I sent him off an hour ago to bring me another panther!"

Moral of this story...

Don't mess with the old dogs: Age and skill will always overcome youth and treachery! ~ Author Unknown

105

Two Traveling Angels

Two traveling angels stopped to spend the night in the home of a wealthy family.

The family was rude and refused to let the angels stay in the mansion's guest room. Instead the angels were given a small space in the cold basement.

As they made their bed on the hard floor, the older angel saw a hole in the wall and repaired it.

When the younger angel asked why, the older angel replied, "Things aren't always what they seem."

The next night the pair came to rest at the house of a very poor, but very hospitable farmer and his wife. After sharing what little food they had, the couple let the angels sleep in their bed where they could have a good night's rest.

When the sun came up the next morning, the angels found the farmer and his wife in tears. Their only cow, whose milk had been their sole income, lay dead in the field.

The younger angel was infuriated and asked the older angel how could you have let this happen? The first man had everything, yet you helped him, she accused.

The second family had little but was willing to share everything, and you let the cow die.

"Things aren't always what they seem," the older angel replied.

"When we stayed in the basement of the mansion, I noticed there was gold stored in that hole in the wall.

Since the owner was so obsessed with greed and unwilling to share his good fortune, I sealed the wall so he wouldn't find it."

"Then last night as we slept in the farmers' bed, the angel of death came for his wife. I gave him the cow instead. Things aren't always what they seem."

Sometimes that is exactly what happens when things don't turn out the way they should. If you have faith, you just need to trust that every outcome is always to your advantage. You just might not know it until sometime later. ~ Author Unknown

Roadblocks

Move those roadblocks aside: That's what successful people didn't do on their quest to achieve their goals:

They didn't try to do it alone. Hence why you have family and friends.

They didn't wait for the "right time" to get started.

They didn't think it would be all fun and fulfillment. Going after your inspirations involves work.

They didn't let their fears get the best of them. We all go through doubts.

They didn't doubt the progress they made. Don't compare yourself to others.

They didn't really see a failure as a failure. Failure leads you to new realms of possibilities.

They never forgot that they had a gift to give. Pursuing your dreams is a personal contribution to life.

Success is a ladder that cannot be climbed with your hands in your pockets. ~ Author Unknown

Taking the Leap of Faith

T he next time you're faced with the dreaded task of speaking in public, remember Eleanor Roosevelt's admonition. The former first lady believed in facing your fears. She once said, "You must do the thing you think you cannot do." For David Roche, that undoable thing must have had a lot to do with appearing in public. Roche was a bright, personable man but he bore what author Gregg Levoy describes as a "striking facial disfigurement."

Levoy relates his first meeting with Roche in his book, "Callings: Finding and Following an Authentic Life."

"My face froze involuntarily into a blank stare, a chink in decorum with which he undoubtedly has a weary familiarity. It took me an egregiously long moment before I recovered from my fumble."

Levoy and Roche were joining several other participants in Lee Glickstein's Speaking Circles, a program created to help people overcome their fear of public speaking.

Needless to say, no one was eager to take the first turn at the podium – no one, that is, except Roche. The audience shifted uncomfortably as the unlikely star stepped onto the makeshift stage. But Roche showed no fear, purposely drawing attention to his disfigurement.

"I was born with a face that's a gift from God," he told the crowd. "Not the kind of gift you rip open exclaiming,

'How exquisite. How did you know?' More like, 'Oh, you shouldn't have.'" The startled audience couldn't help but laugh at Roche's self-deprecating humor. Roche went on to explain that he conquered his fears by remembering that his gift was "to remind people of what they already know – that it's OK to be flawed."

Don't worry so much when you are continually faced with a problem.

1. Identify the problem being faced.
2. Determine the cause of the problem.
3. List all potential solutions to the problem.
4. Choose the best COA to implement.

~ Author Unknown

The Biggest Obstacles
are Always Psychological
and Not Physical

At times I feel overwhelmed when I'm running long distance or pushing myself more than I'm used to. The next time you feel overwhelmed by the sheer height of a figurative mountain, try coming back to the moment. Don't look up. Just take the step in front of you, and the one after that, and the one after that. When you do finally turn and look back at where you started, I think you'll be amazed at how high you've climbed.

Each of us can conquer our own figurative mountain armed with the willingness to take the thousands of small steps needed to reach the top. The biggest obstacles are always psychological and not physical. ~Author Unknown

If you find a path with no obstacles on it, chances are it doesn't lead anywhere. ~ Author Unknown

There are no such things as obstacles in life, only challenges. ~ Joseph Shusko

109

It Pays to Be Kind

For many years, Walter Swords frequented an eatery in a small Texas town. He had a reputation for being foul-mouthed, belligerent and picky.

Melina Salazar describes Swords as "kind of mean." She would know. For almost seven years, she waited on Swords whenever he came into the diner. Despite his ill temper, Salazar was always pleasant to him. She made sure his food was hot and just the way he liked it. And she gave him a big smile with every order.

One day, it dawned on Salazar that Swords hadn't been in the diner for a while. She understood why when she happened across his obituary in the newspaper.

Several months later, Salazar was informed that her former customer had bequeathed her $50,000 and his car. Those who had known the cantankerous Swords were stunned by his posthumous act of generosity.

But why such a surprise? We all have potential to be kind – even those of us who never seem to be anything but miserable and disagreeable. And we have a range of ways to express our kindness: a smile, a touch, a supportive word whispered in hard times. Whether or not the kindness we give is returned or acknowledged is irrelevant. Being kind is a worthy endeavor simply because it's always appreciated – sometimes more than we know. ~ Author Unknown

110

How Heavy are Your Potatoes?

A teacher once told each of her students to bring a clear plastic bag and a 10-pound sack of potatoes to school. For every person they refuse to forgive in their life's experience (whether the person was dead or alive), they chose a potato, wrote on it the name and date, and put in the plastic bag.

Some of their bags were quite heavy. They were then told to carry this bag with them everywhere for two months, putting it beside their beds at night, on the car seat when driving, next to their desk at work, and even on dates. The hassle of lugging this around with them made it clear what a weight they were carrying spiritually and mentally, and how they had to pay attention to it all the time.

Naturally, the condition of the potatoes deteriorated to a nasty smelly slime.

This was a great metaphor for the price we pay for keeping our pain and heavy negativity. Too often we think of forgiveness as a gift to the other person, when it clearly is for ourselves! ~ Author Unknown

111

Let Go of that Grudge

Have you had a negative interaction at work with someone, and now you're holding a grudge? If so, you should probably work through it. Why? Devoting so much time to negative energy is probably not going to pan out for you in the end. Don't get caught in obsessing on what has happened in the past. You can think about it, acknowledge it and even remember it so that you are not vulnerable, but to focus you energies on your grudge will probably only hurt you in the workplace.

If you catch yourself going over and over the offending scenario in your head, take a walk or immerse yourself in some activity that will clear your mind.
~ Author Unknown

Don't carry a grudge. While you're carrying a grudge, the other guy's out dancing. ~ Buddy Hackett

My Father-in-Law

My father-in-law is a plumber and air conditioning guy who is a super hard working son of a gun. He was diagnosed with throat cancer and survived. The family was swamped with medical bills but never declare bankruptcy.

His truck kept breaking down and on a lark he stopped by a Ford dealership on the way home from church just to daydream. The salesman, of course, took him in and convinced him to fill out the paper work "just to see what they say," knowing that his credit was trashed and he couldn't afford a new truck even if they approved him.

The Ford Motor credit manager for Texas called back while they were waiting and asked "Is this the same Ron Hawk who lives In Lake Country?" Yes was the reply. "Well, ask him how many trucks he would like and give him the best deal." Ron signed the paper work and bought 10 trucks, filled them with plumbers and air conditioning techs and now runs a very successful 30 employee business.

The manager who approved his credit was at his dad's house for Christmas one year with all the different family members when the hot water heater went out. The manager's father called Ron who came over and installed a new hot water heater at 11:30 p.m. on Christmas Eve.

He never forgot that and knew he would be good for the loan. That day changed his life from just surviving to being a leading business man in the area. I'm very proud of him. He is my hero and I use him often in my motivational speeches. ~ LtCol "Taco" Bell

113

Shift Your Focus

We often rack our brains to come up with answers or solutions to the problems that face us. We stare at the challenge so hard that we're blinded by it. Sometimes it takes a step back or a look away to get to solutions.

Think of, for example, when you want to see an object in the dark. You'll see it only by looking next to the object, not by looking at it directly.

It's the same as when you try to walk across a room with a full cup of coffee. If you orient yourself to the cup of coffee, you're orienting yourself to a moving target – thus, making an unsteady trek to your desk. But if you look up and orient yourself to your surroundings, you keep your balance smooth and the coffee makes it to your desk without a drop spilled.

So remember to shift your focus the next time a daunting problem or overwhelming situation is before you. The answers you need might be just out of the main view. ~ Author Unknown

114

Five Questions;
Life Support System

Tom saw Joe at the Post Exchange and raced over to see him. "Do you know what I just heard about your good friend?"

"Before you say another word, answer this," said Joe. "Is what you are about to tell be the truth?"

Tom pondered the question for a moment. "I'm not sure, but…"

"Now hold on a minute," said Joe. "Since you don't know whether or not it's true, let me ask you another question. Is this information you have good news?"

"Oh, not at all," said Tom. "In fact…"

"Wait! I have another question," said Joe. "Is what you have to say something that is going to be useful in any way to me?"

"Well," said Tom as his cheeks reddened, "I doubt it."

"So, if it's not true, good news, or anything that would be of use to me, why are you so eager to repeat it? And what makes you think I'd want to hear it?" ~ Author Unknown

Only you can be yourself. No one else is qualified for the job. ~ Author Unknown

Sometimes we have it within ourselves to liberate our spirits from the darkness, though we may need a gentle nudge in the right direction. ~ Author Unknown

Every time you speak, your mind is on parade.
~ Author Unknown

115

Character is:

Competence
Honesty
Assertiveness
Reputation
Attitude
Courage
Tact
Energy
Responsibility

~ Joseph Shusko

116

The Power to Create Change

Have you ever been in a situation that had you so frustrated you were ready to just throw in the towel? Well, the next time you're at your wits end, remember this story.

At the age of 19, Kristin had grown tired of her school. She was offended by some of the "unprofessional" comments of her fellow classmates, and she decided she was going to leave school and attend another school.

"You're going to do what?" her father asked. He'd pulled over the car to the side of the road and turned to face his daughter. Kristin explained her dilemma, but her father was less than sympathetic. He was the kind of man who was big on personal responsibility.

He told Kristin that if she wasn't happy with her school, it was up to her to do something about it. So Kristin had a meeting with her superintendent. She discussed the issues and ways to improve the "unprofessional" comments expressed by her fellow classmates.

That experience taught Kristin that the power to create a change lies in the amount of effort one is willing to invest in the outcome of what they want to achieve.

You don't have to wait for permission to make something happen; you just have to want things to be better than they are. ~ Author Unknown

There are some things that no amount of education or training can prepare you for. Experience is still the best teacher. ~ Author Unknown

If you burn your bridges, make sure you can swim. ~ African proverb

Coming together is a beginning; staying together is progress; working together is success. ~ Henry Ford

117

Balance Your Eggs

A group of people held a banquet for Christopher Columbus shortly after he returned from "discovering" the Americas. After dinner, one of the guests challenged Columbus by saying, "Anyone could have found the Americas," and that Columbus had no "special skills to help him achieve his historical find."

Columbus picked up a hard-boiled egg from the table, and asked the gentleman who had challenged him to balance the egg on its narrow end. The man tried unsuccessfully, and pretty soon the entire party had joined in. Nobody could do it.

Finally, after everyone agreed it was an impossible task, Columbus took the egg, cracked the tip of it slightly, and flattened out the narrow end a little. Then, he easily balanced the egg on the table. Of course, there was an uproar as all the guests claimed that any one of them could have also tapped the top of the egg to balance it. Columbus made his point: Of course any of them could have done it, but none of them did. He said the same thing could be said about discovering the New World.

Although we are all capable, few of us actually use the available knowledge to reach our goals. ~ Christopher Columbus

118

When Energy Ebbs,
Try Something New

When you're feeling low energy and overwhelmed by your life, you might be stifled by your routine. If you are, you might benefit from the following exercise.

Get the local paper that lists what's going on in your town, or the town nearest where you live. Pick out five things that sound like something you'd never do. For instance, if you're not a theatergoer, pick out a live show. If you're not an art aficionado, select an art exhibit to attend. The whole idea is to get your energy flowing in a new direction. You might be surprised how enjoyable these things that you would not normally do, might be. ~ Author Unknown

There is only one endeavor in which you can start at the top, and that's digging a hole. ~ Author Unknown

Try to use the words "I choose to" instead of "I have to" and your life will be different. ~ Author Unknown

119

A True Winner

In the 1950s, Evelyn Ryan was an industrious housewife. She once worked at a local paper but gave that up to start her family. In all, she had 10 children. With such a large brood there never seemed to be enough to make ends meet.

Since working outside the home would've made it impossible to care for her children, Ryan found a way to provide for them from within.

In those days, advertisers sponsored contests to promote products. Evelyn entered these contests with the hopes of winning the things her family needed. She saved more than box tops and proofs-of-purchases. Evelyn wrote poems, jingles, promo ads, and essays – anything that was required for the shot at the grand prize.

She kept detailed notes on what types of entries the agencies responded to and kept a spiral notebook handy to jot down her ideas.

Throughout the years, Evelyn won large and small appliances, two cars, and enough cash to use as a down payment on a house and pay off all her debts. But the most remarkable aspect of Ryan's story is the proof that you can achieve anything when you believe in yourself. ~ Author Unknown

The reason some people don't go very far in life is because they sidestep opportunity and shake hands with procrastination. ~ Author Unknown

120

Full Steam Ahead

When young William Borden – heir to the Borden dairy fortune – graduated from high school more than 100 years ago, his father gave him three things for his graduation gift: enough money for a trip around the world, a servant to accompany him and a brand new Bible.

So at just 16 years of age, William traveled throughout Africa, Asia and the Middle East, experiencing a mix of cultures and people. But the combination of seeing human suffering while simultaneously acquainting himself with the Scriptures caused William's heart to be stirred with a calling from God.

He committed his life to prepare for the mission field, and he wrote two words in the back of his Bible: "No reserve."

Returning home, he enrolled at Yale University, where his spiritual devotion and his ministry to the poor and destitute became well known among the students, faculty and community in New Haven. And though he was courted by both Wall Street and the family business upon graduation, he stayed firm in his desire to serve God overseas.

During this time he wrote two additional words in the back of his Bible: "No retreat."

While traveling through Egypt on his way to a mission in China, William contracted a form of spinal meningitis. Within a month, he died. He was only 25.

Weeks later, as his father was going through William's things, he came across the Bible he had given his son as a high-school graduation present. The list of short handwritten statements in the back now included a third: "No regrets."

No reserve. No retreat. No regrets. Those six words should challenge all of us to be radical followers of Christ.

We should live purposefully in our marriages and families, investing ourselves wholeheartedly in the primary people God has given us to love and to lead. Always forward. Always faithful. No going back. ~ Proverbs 16:3

121

A Family Visit

An elderly man living on the West Coast calls his son living on the East Coast and says, "I have some bad news to share with you. Your mother and I are divorcing."

The son responds, "Pop, that's insane? You can't divorce mom after all these years."

To which the older man replies, "It may sound crazy to you, but 45 years of misery is enough for me. I am going to tell her tomorrow on Thanksgiving Day! It will be the last one we spend together!"

Frantically, the son calls his sister in the Midwest and gives her the news. The sister shouts furiously, "Like heck they're getting a divorce. We're both going to fly out there tomorrow and talk some sense into dad! I don't care if it is Thanksgiving!" She hangs up the phone and calls her parents.

When her father answers the phone she yells, "Don't you dare do a thing until my brother and I get there tomorrow." The old man hangs up his phone and turns to his wife. "Well that's settled," he says with a smile. "They're coming for Thanksgiving and paying their own way. Now what do we tell them for Christmas?" ~ Author Unknown

122

Friend or Foe /
Gullah People of the
US Coastal South (folktale)

Cy the Snail was best pals with Herman, a Crab, even though Herman constantly teased Cy for being slow. "Try to keep up unless you like walking in my shadow," he would taunt.

"I move at my own pace," Cy would reply.

"The good thing is, from here, I can watch your back and warn you if someone is trying to sneak up on you."

"Whatever," Cy would counter. "I'm still your best buddy."

One day, Herman suggested that he and Cy leave the ocean and explore the beach. "My mom doesn't want me to go there," Cy said. "She says the gulls will snatch me away and eat me for dinner."

"And do you always do everything your mother says? Don't be such a bore."

"I am not. . ."

"Tell you what. If you go with me, you can walk in front while I watch your back to make sure the gulls keep their distance." Against his better judgment, Cy agreed and off they went to the beach. Once there, Cy forgot all about what his mother had said. The beach was a whole now frontier for the young snail.

He turned to say something to Herman, but saw Herman running away. And then Cy froze as a huge gull swooped toward him. The last thing Herman saw as he frantically burrowed into the sand was his friend being plucked from the beach by a gull.

How would he ever explain this to Cy's family? He thought and thought. It took him until nightfall to devise a clever-enough lie.

He knocked on the door of his friend's house. When it opened, Herman fainted. Minutes later, he came to and Cy was sitting beside him. "Cy, I didn't think I'd ever see you again."

"Save it," Cy snapped. "Mr. Gull warned me about so-called friends like you."

"Mr. Gull?" Herman queried. "What are you talking about?"

"Mr. Gull picked me up and took me to a clearing. He scolded me for being careless and out of my element. He asked me what would make me want to roam the beach by myself."

"Are you serious?"

"Yes," said Cy. "I told him that I wasn't alone; I was with you. But he said I was as good as alone with someone like you. He advised me to be more selective in choosing my friends."

"Surely, you're not taking that gull seriously. He's a stranger! Our enemy! I'm your best buddy – have been for years."

"Well, it was our enemy who made sure I got home safely," said Cy. "My so-called friend left me when I needed him most." ~ Author Unknown

123

The Mask of Happiness

Long ago, a short-tempered and ill-mannered King was miserable. Yet, he yearned to be happy. It posed such a challenge to him that he sent for the kingdom's wizard, his most loyal and trusted advisor.

"I want my life to be filled with joy and happiness," the king explained. "And you must help me achieve this."

"As you wish, Your Majesty." And the wizard left.

A few days later, the sage returned with a solution. "If you want to be happy, Your Majesty, you must act happy and pleasant," he said. "And you must wear this mask." The wizard handed the king a mask that was a copy of the king's face – except with a more pleasant countenance. The king put on the mask and as he walked around the castle, he noticed that people always smiled back at him. This delighted the king. He wasn't used to his subjects responding to him so positively.

Soon he began to interact more closely with the members of his court. He grew to know and appreciate them, and they came to know and respect him.

However, after a year, the king grew troubled. "Though this mask has greatly improved my life, I can no longer continue deceiving the good people of this kingdom," the king confessed one day to his wizard. "I must remove this mask and reveal my true self to my subjects - even if it means losing their respect."

"As you wish, Your Majesty," the wizard replied and guided the king to a mirror. When the king removed the mask, he discovered that his once-wrinkled brow was now smooth. And the scowl he'd worn on his face in the "pre-mask" days was gone. His lips were curved in a pleasant smile; his face now resembled the mask he'd worn for the last year.

"This is remarkable," exclaimed the king. "I am a new person!"

"This is who you really are, Your Majesty," assured the wizard. "You just needed to be reminded." ~ Author Unknown

124

Integrity Always Pays Off

Gabrielle Melchionda started making all natural lip balm to give away to friends and her hobby soon turned into a full time business.

Eventually, she was offered what seemed like the deal of a lifetime. An exporter was willing to give her a contract for $2 million to sell her lip balms internationally. But for Gabrielle there was one huge problem. This same exporter also sold weapons, and she didn't feel good about that.

Ultimately, Gabrielle passed on the opportunity to expand her business through that partnership.

Since then, she's never looked back. Profits have grown, and so has her company. Business is so good that she had to move her company into a larger office and production facility. Her line has expanded to sell body balms, sunscreen and soy candles. Her products are carried by major retailers around the country.

It pays to stick to your principles. Success is the reward for those who are willing to work hard at what they believe in and not compromise when it comes to things that they don't. ~ Author Unknown

Offering someone your undivided attention is one of the greatest honors you can bestow upon them. ~ Author Unknown

The shortest and surest way to live with honor in the world is to be in reality what we would appear to be; and if we observe, we shall find that all human virtues increase and strengthen themselves by the practice and experience of them. ~ Socrates

Hope Defined: Balances out all the negative things in life. It means a helpful optimism promoting equilibrium. ~ Author Unknown

125

Feeling What's Empty /
Power of Paradox

A Zen master took on a new student who had previously studied under several other masters. During their first encounter the student began to speak of his past studies and achievements. The master listened patiently until a servant appeared with a tray of tea.

"Please pour the tea," the master instructed his apprentice. "I will tell you when to stop." The student eagerly seized the teapot and began to pour the tea into the master's cup. As the cup began to fill, the student began to slow his pour. "Keep pouring," the master instructed as the tea spilled over the sides of the cup and onto the floor. "But the cup is full," the student objected as he drained the pot.

"The tea has been wasted. You have a lot in common with this cup," said the master. "You are already so full of knowledge that there is no room for more. Would my wisdom be wasted on you?"

The student looked down at his feet. "Don't despair. There is still hope," suggested the master as he poured out the tea from the cup onto the floor. "An empty cup can hold more than one that is already full."

Sometimes in order to learn what you need to know, you need to forget what you think you know. ~ Author Unknown

Thoughts are like arrows: Once released, they strike their mark. Guard them well, or one day you may be your own victim. ~ Navajo Proverb

126

A Deal's a Deal

When Josh received his driver's license he approached his father about using the family car regularly. "Driving is a huge responsibility," said his father, "and one that I don't want you to take lightly. But I'll make a deal with you. If you bring your grades up, start helping around the house more, go to church with your mom and me, and cut your hair, we can work something out about you getting some time with the car."

"Okay," agreed Josh. And for the next few weeks he devoted more time to his schoolwork and chores, and he attended church every Sunday with his parents.

"All Bs and one C," Josh boasted as he handed over his grades from the quarter.

"Good effort," his father said. "I'm proud of you."

"So now can we talk about me using the car?"

"Not so fast, "said his father. "We had a deal remember? Grades, chores, church, and hair?"

"Dad, come on. Do I really have to cut my hair? It took me so long to grow it out. Besides, Samson had long hair. Moses had long hair. And Jesus had long hair," said Josh.

"You're right," agreed his father. "And guess what? They walked everywhere they went." ~ Author Unknown

A person wrapped up in himself makes for a very small bundle. ~ Benjamin Franklin

No difficult or simple job ever gets done until someone decides right now to do what it takes to get the job done. Unfortunately, too many people stand by ready to carry the stool when there is a piano to be moved. ~ Herbert. Hoover

127

Compassion Opens the Door to Worlds of Possibilities

Two men once took on the challenge of coaching a ninth-grade wrestling team. They agreed that they would include as many prospects who exhibited a certain level of skill. They believed that their goal was to not only develop a team of strong wrestlers, but also the self-esteem of a group of young men.

Of all the prospects, four were not good enough to make the team. Instead of just releasing them from the roster, each of the four were pulled aside by the coaches. Each was offered feedback, and explained the decision not to include them on the team.

Later, the coaches were surprised to receive emails from two of the boys. The teens expressed their appreciation for being given the opportunity to attend the tryouts.

Eventually, three of them continued to practice with the team throughout the season. Too often these probationary periods yield little more than a sense of failure in those who don't make the final cut. But the coaches believed that a more personal approach in dealing with under-performers had long-lasting, positive effects.

By treating these young hopefuls with dignity and respect, the coaches inspired a confidence that gave these kids the courage to move beyond their weaknesses and keep trying. ~ Author Unknown

If someone is going down the wrong road, they don't need motivation to speed them up. What they needs is education to turn them around. ~ Author Unknown

Even our most personal and confidential observances can be aired in front of unintended audiences. It's important to always say what you mean, mean what you say, and be willing to take responsibility for the things you say. I believe that every word we utter is a moral choice. Keep that in mind the next time you speak your mind. ~ Author Unknown

A good example is like a bell that calls many to church. ~ Danish Proverb

128

More Than Meets the Eye

Junior loved to hang out at the corner store, so the manager hired him to do odd jobs such as sweeping and sorting the recycling. Junior was a quiet kid, but a good kid, though he seemed a little different from the other kids his age.

A group of boys who went to school with Junior often teased him when they were in the store. "Two bricks short of a load," they would say. "Which one is more," they would ask and offer him the choice between a dime or a nickel. Junior always chose the nickel and would laugh with them as they called him a sucker.

The manager always scolded the boys for being smart alecks, but Junior seemed oblivious to their pranks. One day, after getting another nickel, the manager finally said to him, "Junior, why do you let those boys make fun of you? A dime is smaller in size, but worth more than a nickel. "I know," said Junior. "But if I take the dime they'll stop giving me the money." ~ Author Unknown

Life is a continuous process of getting used to things we hadn't expected. ~ Author Unknown

Live your life as an exclamation, not an explanation.
~ Isaac Newton

129

Bury Your Self – Pity

The next time you and your colleagues are feeling less than motivated, try this simple activity to boost morale: Sit around a table and create a list of all the things each person feels he or she cannot do. Write out just one master list of these shortcomings on a sheet of 8.5" x 11" paper.

Next, take the list, fold it up, and put it in the bottom of a planter or clay pot. Pour some soil over the list and add a new plant that will thrive in your office environment, dorm, room, etc (taking into consideration, of course, the amount of sunlight your area receives).

Take turns caring for and watering the plant. It will be a nice reminder of things that can be accomplished.

~ Author Unknown

The road to success is dotted with many tempted parking places. ~ Will Rogers

130

When the Going Gets Tough,
Stay Put

There once lived a man who left his home and headed west toward his dreams. His sights were set on making his fortune in gold. He soon discovered a vein of ore in some hills and settled there. The vein was plentiful. In no time at all, the man had enough gold to purchase the equipment that would help him mine all the ore from the vein.

All went well for the prospector until one day, the vein unexpectedly dried up. No matter how hard he tried, the man couldn't find any more gold. So he gave up his dreams and decided to leave while he still had a shirt on his back.

He sold his claim and equipment to a junk dealer and headed back east. The junk dealer wanted to know just what he'd bought and hired a mining expert to survey the claim.

The expert said there was nothing at all wrong with the vein. It had simply shifted a few feet away from its original position due to a fault line. The junk dealer began prospecting and became one of the wealthiest men in the area. Most of his neighbors envied his luck. But the junk dealer knew it was more than luck that make him rich. He understood that discarded dreams are always filled with treasures for those who will pick them up and carry them to fruition. ~ Author Unknown

Good things require time. ~ Dutch Proverb

Every hour misspent is lost forever. ~ George Washington

Patience is ointment for every sore. ~ Welsh Proverb

131

No One is Perfect

All things in the world are two. In our minds we are two: good and evil. With our eyes we see two things: things that are fair and things that are ugly. We have the right hand that strikes and makes for evil, and the left hand full of kindness near the heart.

One foot may lead us to an evil way; the other foot may lead us to a good. So are all things two, all two.
~ Eagle Chief

132

Activating Core Values

No matter what we feel or know, no matter what our potential gifts or talents, only action brings them to life. Many of us understand concepts such as Honor, Courage and Commitment, but we truly know only when we can do. Doing leads to understanding, and action turns knowledge into wisdom. ~ Author Unknown

We are all born with two ends: one to think with and one to sit on. Success in life depends mainly on which of these you use the most; and it is a toss-up, heads you win, tails you lose. ~ Author Unknown

133

It's What You Scatter

I was at the corner grocery store buying some early potatoes. I noticed a small boy, delicate of bone and feature, ragged but clean, hungrily apprising a basket of freshly picked green peas.

I paid for my potatoes but was also drawn to the display of fresh green peas. I am a pushover for creamed peas and new potatoes. Pondering the peas, I couldn't help overhearing the conversation between Mr. Miller (the store owner) and the ragged boy next to me. "Hello Barry, how are you today?"

"Hello, Mr. Miller. Fine, thank ya. Jus' admirin' them peas. They sure look good."

"They are good, Barry. How's your Ma?"

"Fine. Gittin' stronger alla' time."

"Good. Anything I can help you with?"

"No, Sir. Jus' admirin' them peas."

"Would you like to take some home?" asked Mr. Miller.

"No, Sir. Got nuthin' to pay for 'em with."

"Well, what have you to trade me for some of those peas?"

"All I got's my prize marble here."

Is that right? Let me see it," said Miller.

"Here 'tis. She's a dandy."

"I can see that. Hmmmmm, only thing is this one is blue and I sort of go for red. Do you have a red one like this at home?" the store owner asked.

"Not zackley but almost."

"Tell you what. Take this sack of peas home with you and next trip this way let me look at that red marble." Mr. Miller told the boy.

"Sure will. Thanks Mr. Miller."

Mrs. Miller, who had been standing nearby, came over to help me. With a smile she said, "There are two other boys like him in our community, all three are in very poor circumstances. Jim just loves to bargain with them for peas, apples, tomatoes or whatever. When they come back with their red marbles, and they always do, he decides he doesn't like red after all and he sends them home with a bag of produce for a green marble or an orange one, when they come on their next trip to the store."

I left the store smiling to myself, impressed with this man. A short time later I moved to Colorado, but I never forgot the story of this man, the boys, and their bartering for marbles.

Several years went by, each more rapid than the previous one. Just recently I had occasion to visit some old friends in that Idaho community and while I was there learned that Mr. Miller had died. They were having his visitation that evening and knowing my friends wanted to go, I agreed to accompany them.

Upon arrival at the mortuary we fell into line to meet the relatives of the deceased and to offer whatever words of comfort we could. Ahead of us in line were three young men. One was in an army uniform and the other two wore nice haircuts, dark suits and white shirts...all very professional looking. They approached Mrs. Miller, standing composed and smiling by her husband's casket. Each of the young men hugged her, kissed her on the cheek, spoke briefly with her and moved on to the casket.

Her misty light blue eyes followed them as, one by one; each young man stopped briefly and placed his own warm hand over the cold pale hand in the casket. Each left the mortuary awkwardly, wiping his eyes.

Our turn came to meet Mrs. Miller. I told her who I was and reminded her of the story from those many years ago and what she had told me about her husband's bartering for marbles. With her eyes glistening, she took my hand and led me to the casket. "Those three young men who just left were the boys I told you about. They just told me how they appreciated the things Jim 'traded' them. Now, at last, when Jim could not change his mind about color or size....they came to pay their debt. We've never had a great deal of the wealth of this world," she confided, "but right now, Jim would consider himself the richest man in Idaho." With loving gentleness she lifted the lifeless fingers of her deceased husband. Resting underneath were three exquisitely shined red marbles.

The Moral: We will not be remembered by our words, but by our kind deeds. Life is not measured by the breaths we take, but by the moments that take our breath. Today I wish you a day of ordinary miracles. A fresh pot of coffee you didn't make yourself... An unexpected phone call from an old friend ... Green stoplights on your way to work ...The fastest line at the grocery store ... A good sing-along song on the radio ...Your keys found right where you left them. ~ Author Unknown

A simple smile is a universal language ~ think about it. Always meet people fully dressed; with a smile.
~ Joe Shusko

134

One of Those Days

The staff at the coffee shop was having "one of those days." The espresso machine was malfunctioning; the bakery had not delivered the bagels and sweet rolls; someone from the morning shift called in sick; and the crew from the previous evening failed to restock the cabinets with supplies. There were several people waiting to get their 1st cup of Joe (coffee).

A woman at the back of the line began to complain loudly. "What is taking so long? Are you growing the beans back there? I don't have all day!"

"Yes, we are running on empty this morning," the manager said with a smile. He motioned for the woman to come forward. "What can I get for you?"

"I want a large coffee with steamed milk to go," barked the lady.

"No problem," said the manager. He looked past the woman to the other customers waiting in line and offered them a reassuring wink. In a matter of moments he had made the woman's coffee, took her money, and sent her on her way. "Have a nice day," the manager said to the woman. The other customers stood silently with confused looks on their faces.

The manager said, "Folks, I'm really sorry for the inconvenience this morning. Because you have been so patient, your coffee is on the house." ~ Author Unknown

135

Grab the Handle of Success

Frank Miles is an acrobat, a magician and a juggler. He's entertained audiences in Los Vegas, appeared on TV, and inspired people around the world to conquer their fears to achieve success. It may come as a surprise to learn that Miles was quite awkward and shy as a teenager. What brought him out of his shell was learning how to juggle. As his skills developed, so did his self-confidence. When Miles realized how comfortable he felt performing for his friends, he found the courage to do his act in front of strangers.

Though juggling might seem difficult to some of us, Miles believes it's easy. The key is to focus your attention on the handle of the object you want to catch. Miles equates success in life with juggling. He says, "Everything you encounter in life has a handle, a place where you can act or react to it. The other end – what we often call the result – is the blade. I learned that my fear of others resulted from my habit of focusing on how I wanted them to feel, think or act. My attentions and efforts were directed at that blade, over which I had no real control."

Always remember that you have the greatest amount of control over what's in your hand. Focus your attention on the handle to grab a hold of success. ~ Author Unknown

136

Cut Time

Eubie Blake was considered by many to be the father of rag time. His career spanned from adolescence well into his middle age.

After more than 20 years in retirement, he decided to record an album and hit the scene again. He would perform for more than a decade making his last musical appearance just before his 100th birthday.

Throughout his career many in the jazz world would seek him out for advice. "I want to write a musical score," an aspiring composer said to Blake. "Can you tell me how to do it?"

"You're very young," Blake said. "You should wait a few years, when you're a little older." Blake said.

"But you were composing when you were in your teens, much younger than I am now," said the man.

"This is true," Blake replied, "but I didn't have to ask anyone how to do it."

If you've got the passion, you don't need anyone's permission or guidance to bring your dreams to fruitions. All you need to do is roll up your sleeves and get to work.
~ Author Unknown

137

Be Yourself

A young man was preparing for his first job interview. His friends gave him advice on what to wear, how to act, and what to say. "Don't laugh or smile. Be serious," they told him. "It will make you seem more sophisticated."

He arrived for his interview 15 minutes early and was greeted by a cheerful woman standing at the front desk. He told her who he was and why he was there. She promptly escorted him to a conference room and offered him a cup of coffee. He decided to ask her a few questions about the job, hoping a brief exchange with a neutral person would calm his nerves. She offered him insight on the position and in turn asked him about his education. Their conversation flowed naturally and he hoped that the real interview would go as well. Finally the woman looked at her watch and said, "You're punctual, enthusiastic, easy to talk to, and with your background you'd make an excellent employee here. When can you start?"

"What?" said the young man.

"The job is yours if you want it," said the woman. He stared at her for a moment; then she said, "Oh, my goodness, I was so preoccupied thinking about our receptionist who is out sick today that I never introduced myself. I'm Ms. Smith from Human Resources. We spoke on the phone earlier."

The young man was astonished. He'd just landed his first job doing everything his friends told him not to do. It pays to be yourself. ~ Author Unknown

Only you can be yourself. No one else is qualified for the job. ~Author Unknown

138

Inspiring Thoughts to Live By

Live the life you had planned for as long as you can.
Don't be shy about asking for help.
Avoid shutting out others.

Beware of self-pity.

Find your community.

Don't feel obligated to tell everyone about your condition.

Appreciate yourself for who you are.

Know that you can be happy. ~ Author Unknown

139

The Poor Farmer Story

The country was in East Asia. There was much denigration of the country by the local American military people because the people were very poor and the whole country, well, in the inimitable G.I. vernacular, "smelled like crap." Why did the country smell so bad to us Americans? The answer: The local farmers used human waste on their acres and acres of vegetable gardens. There was a constant, heavy, choking odor to the air.

The farms around the main highways used by the Americans were causing the main problem. Dr. Robert Humphrey, conflict resolution expert, set out with an interpreter to see if the local farmers would use more modern methods of composting to reduce the smell if the Americans paid the costs.

The first farmer was willing, but the social amenities necessary for such a delicate and sensitive discussion took almost the entire day.

On the second day, the interpreter stopped the car on the side of the road to go in and arrange an interview with the second farmer. Anticipating a long wait, similar to the previous day, Humphrey pulled out a novel and began to read. He was surprised, therefore when the interpreter returned before he could finish two pages. The interpreter, Mr. Oh, was laughing and shaking his head.

"What's the matter?" asked Humphrey. "Well," Mr. Oh said, "The farmer insisted that I bring you a message. But first, I might mention that you will want to remember this experience to use the next time an American makes the familiar mistake of thinking that all Asians only tell you what you want to hear."

"Sounds like he might have said no to the compost idea," Humphrey observed.

Still smiling, Mr. Oh explained, "I had just finished the introductory comments about the importance of good relations and the mutual struggle against communism, and had turned carefully to a mention of the smell – the fertilizer. He stopped me from speaking further by holding up both hands the way some Americans do."

"'All right, all right,' he said to me. 'I saw you drive up. I thought that was a big nose [American] in the car. I see them drive by here all the time with those long noses in the air or making a big show of holding them. Well, please, I want you to go back to your American friend and tell him these exact words for me. Tell him and all your American bosses that I have five children to feed. Tell them that I can't afford any other kind of fertilizer, and I don't want to take chances with any other kind. Tell them that if my crop fails, these children will starve. One winter their bellies swelled up with hunger. Tell them that, after that terrible year, every time I come out of this house in the morning and I smell that stuff, it just smells great! I suck it down into my lungs and say to myself: OH! THAT JUST SMELLS GREAT! In fact, when I don't smell that wonderful smell, it makes me feel sick. So go! Tell him; tell them. We have nothing more to discuss.'" ~ Dr. Robert Humphrey, *Values For A New Millennium*

140

Another "Iwo Jima Story"

In one rifle platoon, two of the teenage Marines had "stressed-out" after 34 of their 40 man platoon had been shot in the first five days. The two were no longer staying alert. Robert Humphrey, the lieutenant in charge, warned them that the Japanese would soon sneak into their fox holes, beat them to a shot and kill them. They did not respond. He raged at them, repeatedly, with the same warning about their impending death. It still did not work. One of the platoon's wiser young riflemen, son of a Texas rancher, advised Humphrey quietly that he was telling the men the wrong thing. He said, "Tell them, Lieutenant that the Japanese will get past them and kill others." To Humphrey's shock, that worked. ~ Dr. Robert Humphrey, *Values For A New Millennium*

141

The Baboon Story

aby baboons make the favorite meals for the big cats. When a troop of baboons is foraging, they stay in military formation so that all the males can gang-up on, and drive off, a leopard that is seeking a feast. But this day, an old leopard had surprised a troop of baboons just as it was breaking up the formation to make camp for the night. The hungry leopard was gathering himself for his attack while arrogantly ignoring two (only two) old male baboons that were edging along an overhanging cliff just above him. Two baboons are too few, by several, to cope with the powerful slashing teeth and claws of the hungry killer-cat. Nonetheless, on this day, the two males dropped in attack. One bit at the leopard's spine the other struck at his throat. The leopard instantly killed them both, but it was too late. The dying disemboweled baboon on the leopard's neck had hung on just long enough and had bitten through to the juggler vein. And, somewhat in triumph for all the underdogs of life, a society of animals settled down safely, that night, to sleep.

Remember, our Human Equality comes from the Life Value, and the Life Value is a dual value: self and others.

Robert Humphrey observes:

1. The way you can get yourself into the second most danger – of all possible ways, everywhere in this world, with most persons in the world – is to threaten their lives.

2. Now (to test your understanding of life's controlling value) if that is the second most dangerous action you can take, what is the most dangerous?

Yes, of course, to threaten their loved-ones' lives.

~ Robert Ardrey, *Territorial Imperative*

142

The Iwo Jima Story II

I took over my platoon in a protected area. Men were walking around. They were an experienced, confident group who had been involved in the fighting at the top of Mount Suribachi – site of the famous Iwo Jima flag raising.

One young man was especially noticeable, carrying an unusual Thompson submachine gun. He oozed self-confidence and independence. After chow that first evening, as he perfected his foxhole, he started declaring to himself in a loud voice, "I don't volunteer for nothin' else! Screw the Marine Corps! Screw Mount Suribachi! Screw everything except ol' number one! That's all that counts: gettin' off this island alive! I don't volunteer for nothin'!"

He shouted it so repeatedly that a couple of the other men picked it up. "Yeah! Right! We don't volunteer for nothing!" Suddenly it dawned on me that they were obliquely speaking to me, their new platoon leader. I felt the chill of having my leadership threatened.

The next morning, as we prepared to edge out of our positions, a message came down from higher headquarters. As luck would have it, I was being ordered to send a volunteer out onto a hill in front of us on a sure-death reconnaissance mission. Hesitant to ask for volunteers after what I had heard the night before, I announced that I, myself would go. I made the excuse that, since I was new, I wanted to see the terrain. No sooner had

I spoken, than the same Marine who had made the declarations the previous night said, "No, I'll go, Lieutenant."

"What!" I exclaimed. "You were the one with the big mouth saying that you never volunteer for anything!"

Almost sheepishly trying to cover his willingness to take my place, he answered, "Well, I just can't trust any of these other jarheads on such a mission."

In murderous combat during World War II, Humphrey found that as the fatalities mounted in his platoon, the men began to question and denounce the cultural values that they were being asked to die for: honor, country, democracy, the Marine Corps, etc. However, when he had to appoint someone to an almost suicide mission to save the others, he was stunned to see that, if he did not select the best man for that particular death-mission, one or another of the men who knew himself to be better for the task was prone to volunteer in these terms, "My turn, Lieutenant." This was not only stunning, Humphrey observed, but awe-inspiring because it was always clear what these men were routinely saying, in fact: "My turn (to die), Lieutenant, not his," or in the case above, "Lieutenant, not yours." ~ Dr. Robert Humphrey, *Values For A New Millennium*

143

Leading Ethically – From the Bottom Up

So, what if you are not in a leadership position – yet? Often, as followers or employees or plain old citizens, we are confronted with ethical deficiencies in our leaders that we feel powerless to address without getting ourselves in trouble or fired. Sometimes we have to leave a job that pressures us to be unethical and/or participate in unethical corporate behaviors, particularly if we are dealing with a sociopathic boss. That takes...courage. But not all bad bosses are sociopaths. Some just don't have a reliable moral compass that functions well under stress. You might be able to help them.

The best way to help them is to model ethical behavior yourself, and inspire them with your own words and actions – and sometimes a little cleverness. ~ Jack Hoban, *The Ethical Warrior*

144

The King, Bazgul
and the Innkeeper

Have you ever heard the story of Bazgul Badakhshi? He was a very famous Afghan folk musician who lived to the age of 105. When Afghanistan was still ruled by a King, Bazgul was invited to the capital, Kabul, to perform at the palace. Bazgul was not a rich man; he had no money to pay for a hotel after a long trip from the north. He was not worried, however, because he had been promised a respectable fee for his performance. He arrived in Kabul the night before he was to sing and checked in to a modest hotel, telling the proprietor why he was there, and that he would pay his hotel bill as soon as he was paid by the king.

The next day he performed marvelously, so beautifully, in fact, that the King was overcome by his emotions and forgot to pay Bazgul his fee! Bazgul fretfully went back to the hotel with the bad news. The hotel owner threatened to have Bazgul arrested. But Bazgul had an idea on how to get the money. He shared the plan with the innkeeper who agreed to play his part.

Every day the King would tour the capital in his automobile so that he would be visible to his people. He always took the same route, and that route went right by the hotel where Bazgul was staying.

Sure enough, the next morning the King's car headed down the street toward the inn right on time. As planned, the innkeeper chased Bazgul out of the hotel in front of the King's car, beating the singer about the head and shoulders with a broom yelling, "This man is a thief and a liar!"

The King recognized the man being beaten as Bazgul and had his driver stop the car. The King got out and demanded to know why the innkeeper was beating the beloved singer. The innkeeper repeated that the man was a thief and a liar. The King demanded that the innkeeper explain himself.

"Well, this man stayed at my hotel last night and didn't pay, so he is a thief," said the innkeeper."

"But why is he a liar?" asked the King.

"He is a liar because he told me that he sang for the King last night, and the King did not pay him. Well, that is a lie; because we have only one King in this country and that King is honorable and would never fail to pay a debt!"

The King realized his omission of the night before, was chagrined, paid Bazgul – and the hotel owner – and everyone was happy.

Just as Bazgul helped the King act ethically, we can sometimes do the same thing, but it may require us to be as clever. ~ Author Unknown

145

The Bully

Y ou are a kid in the schoolyard. You see a bully. He sees himself as the "top dog." That perception is a relative value: He may believe it, but everybody else surely doesn't. But, that is fine. Who cares what he thinks? Until the day that his relative value supersedes the Life Value of another kid – in other words, when the bully picks on and/or punches the other kid. This is wrong and must be stopped.

Here is the rule: relative values, no matter how "great," cannot supersede the Life Value.

You see the bully picking on the other kid. You feel – in your gut – that this is wrong. Congratulations, you are moral. By the way, most people are moral – they know the difference between right and wrong and prefer the right.

One day, you see the bully picking on the other kid. You overcome the "freeze," you overcome the embarrassment, and you go tell a teacher. Congratulations! You are ethical. Ethics are moral values in action.

In another scenario, you see the bully picking on the other kid. You overcome the "freeze," you overcome the fear, and you go to the aid of the kid being bullied. You put yourself at risk. Congratulations! You have the makings of an Ethical Warrior. ~ Jack Hoban, *The Ethical Warrior*

146

The Hobo

Making the right choice is not always easy, but please consider the following true story. It was witnessed by the great science fiction writer Robert Heinlein during his childhood; and he told it during a graduation address at his alma mater, the U.S. Naval Academy.

One day while strolling through the great park in Kansas City, he and his mother saw a young woman get her foot caught in the tracks at a railroad crossing. The woman's husband was desperately trying to free her because a train was bearing down on them. The train was travelling far too quickly to stop before the crossing.

As Heinlein and his mother watched the terrifying situation unfold, a hobo suddenly appeared and immediately joined the husband's futile effort to pull the woman free. But tug and twist as they might, they could not get her foot unstuck.

The train killed all three of them.

In his description of the vagabond's effort, Heinlein observed that the hobo did not so much as look up to consider his own escape. Clearly, it was his intention either to save the woman or to die trying. Heinlein concluded his account of the nameless hero's action with this comment: "This is the way a man dies," but he then added, "And this is the way a man lives."

Dr. Robert Humphrey always asked his audiences: What did Heinlein mean when he said, "This is the way a man lives?" After all, he died!

Audiences could seldom fully explain their feelings, but they always realized that the story held meaning for all of our lives. Guided discussion usually revealed that most people thought a noble and generous life was better than a selfish, although possibly longer, one. What do you think?

~ Dr. Robert Humphrey

147

The Corporal
and the Iraqi Funeral Procession

During the early stages of the Iraq War, violence was a daily occurrence and tensions were high between the local populace and the coalition forces. In a rough area outside the main city of Ramadi, a squad of about a dozen Marines, led by a corporal, was on patrol. They became aware of a major disturbance brewing out of sight behind a building about a block away. Suddenly, a large, menacing crowd came around the corner right toward them. Immediately, the Marines went on high alert. The Iraqis were yelling and wailing and a confrontation seemed inevitable. Yet, somehow the corporal sensed that what he was seeing was not an attack on his patrol, but an Iraqi funeral.

Instead of opening fire on the agitated crowd, he ordered his men to ground their weapons, take off their helmets, and bow while the procession passed. An amazing thing happened. Immediately the atmosphere changed, the tension dissipated, and the group passed peaceably. Not only was there no fighting, but that gesture of respect led to good relations between the Marines and the people of that area from then on. ~ Marine Corps Martial Arts Program After Action report

148

Two Days
We Should Not Worry

There are two days in every week about which we
should not worry, two days which should be kept
free from fear and apprehension.

One of these days is yesterday with all its mistakes and
cares, its faults and blunders, its aches and pains.
Yesterday has passed forever beyond our control. All the
money in the world cannot bring back yesterday. We
cannot undo a single act we performed; we cannot erase a
single word we said.

Yesterday is gone forever.

The other day we should not worry about is tomorrow
with all its possible adversities, its burdens, its large
promise and its poor performance. Tomorrow is also
beyond our immediate control.

Tomorrow's sun will rise, either in splendor or behind
a mask of clouds, but it will rise. Until it does, we have no
stake in tomorrow, for it is yet to be born.

This leaves only one day, today. Any person can fight
the battle of just one day. It is when you and I add the
burdens of those two awful eternities–yesterday and
tomorrow – that we break down.

It is not the experience of today that drives a person
mad, it is the remorse or bitterness of something which

happened yesterday and the dread of what tomorrow may bring.

Let us, therefore, live but one day at a time. ~ Author Unknown

149

The Chapters of your Life

I have two arms, two legs, a good heart, and a great mind. I can make my life how I want. Everything in the past is already done. You cannot change the last chapter, for it is already written, but this very second you are writing your book of life. You are in control of your life.

Tired? Go to sleep.

Hungry? Eat.

Fat and lazy? Work out.

Unhappy? Change things so you are happy.

That's like people often ask: What is the best vacation you have been on? What was your favorite day this week? What was your most meaningful experience? All of them are the same.

The next trip I'm planning.

Today is my best day. For tomorrow is no guarantee.

The most meaningful experience is the one I have yet to go on. So since I have the same genetic makeup as someone who is an Olympian, or as Bill Gates, what is the difference between them and I. Absolutely nothing. You hold your book, you write it how you want it to be. ~ SSgt John Trickler USMC

150

The Brick

A brick laid today, build's a solid wall tomorrow. That brick was an obstacle that I doubted myself with. A small action on your part gave me the confidence to finish that wall with one brick at a time.

The darkest part of the day is right before dawn. No sun, no moon, no stars. The sun takes a small action. It gives the world confidence and the sky starts to lighten bringing warmth and light to our eyes and changing the whole day for the better. Every action you take, no matter how small or big, always is a subsequent reaction. A smile, a wave, a pat on the back pushing yourself in part can change the outcome of the day for you but it also impacts many others.

Thanks again for taking that small action. It is it not just to lead, but to mentor, and strive to make your men better. One small action on your part changes the world for others. ~ SSgt John Trickler

151

Now She is a Teacher!

In September of 2005, on the first day of school, Martha Cothren, a history teacher at Robinson High School in Little Rock, Arkansas, did something not to be forgotten. On the first day of school, with the permission of the school superintendent, the principal and the building supervisor, she removed all of the desks in her classroom. When the first period kids entered the room they discovered that there were no desks.

"Ms. Cothren, where are our desks?"

She replied, "You can't have a desk until you tell me how you earn the right to sit at a desk."

They thought, "Well, maybe it's our grades."

"No," she said.

"Maybe it's our behavior."

She told them, "No, it's not even your behavior."

And so, they came and went, the first period, second period, third period. Still no desks in the classroom. Kids called their parents to tell them what was happening and by early afternoon television news crews had started gathering at the school to report about this crazy teacher who had taken all the desks out of her room.

The final period of the day came and as the puzzled students found seats on the floor of the desk-less classroom. Martha Cothren said, "Throughout the day no one has been able to tell me just what he or she has done to earn the right to sit at the desks that are ordinarily found in this classroom. Now I am going to tell you."

At this point, Martha Cothren went over to the door of her classroom and opened it. Twenty-seven (27) U.S. Veterans, all in uniform, walked into that classroom, each one carrying a school desk. The Vets began placing the school desks in rows, and then they would walk over and stand alongside the wall. By the time the last soldier had set the final desk in place those kids started to understand, perhaps for the first time in their lives, just how the right to sit at those desks had been earned.

Martha said, "You didn't earn the right to sit at these desks. These heroes did it for you. They placed the desks here for you. They went halfway around the world, giving up their education and interrupting their careers and families so you could have the freedom you have. Now, it's up to you to sit in them. It is your responsibility to learn, to be good students, to be good citizens. They paid the price so that you could have the freedom to get an education. Don't ever forget it."

By the way, this is a true story. And this teacher was awarded Veterans of Foreign Wars Teacher of the Year for the State of Arkansas in 2006. She is the daughter of a WWII POW.

Let us always remember the men and women of our military and the rights they have won for us. ~ Author Unknown

152

All Things Are Not
What They Seem

The ability to work out what is really happening with a person is simple – not easy, but simple. It's about matching what you see and hear in the environment in which it all happens and drawing probable conclusions. Most people, however, only see the things they think they are seeing.

Here's a story to demonstrate the point:

Two men were walking through the woods when they came across a big deep hole.

'Wow ... that looks deep," says one. "Let's toss a few pebbles in and see how deep it is." They threw in a few pebbles and waited, but there was no sound.

"Gee, that is a really deep hole. Let's throw one of these big rocks in. That should make a noise."

They picked up two football-sized rocks and tossed them into the hole and waited, but still they heard nothing.

"There's a railway sleeper over here in the weeds,' said one. 'If we toss that in, it's definitely going to make some noise."

They dragged the heavy sleeper over to the hole and heaved it in, but not a sound came from the hole.

Suddenly, out of the nearby woods, a goat appeared, running like the wind. It rushed towards the two men and ran right between them, running as fast as its legs could go. Then it leaped into the air and disappeared into the hole. The two men stood there, astonished at what they'd just seen.

Out of the woods came a farmer who said, "Hey! Did you guys see my goat?"

"You bet we did! It was the craziest thing we've ever seen! It came running like the wind out of the woods and jumped into that hole!"

"Nah," says the farmer. "That couldn't have been my goat. My goat was chained to a railway sleeper."

"Wanting people to listen, you can't just tap them on the shoulder anymore. You have to hit them with a sledgehammer, and then you'll notice you've got their strict attention." ~ Author Unknown

153

An Obituary Printed in the London Times

Today we mourn the passing of a beloved old friend, Common Sense, who has been with us for many years. No one knows for sure how old he was, since his birth records were long ago lost in bureaucratic red tape. He will be remembered as having cultivated such valuable lessons as:

- Knowing when to come in out of the rain;
- Why the early bird gets the worm;
- Life isn't always fair;
- And maybe it was my fault.

Common Sense lived by simple, sound financial policies (don't spend more than you can earn) and reliable strategies (adults, not children, are in charge).

His health began to deteriorate rapidly when well-intentioned but overbearing regulations were set in place. Reports of a 6-year-old boy charged with sexual harassment for kissing a classmate; teens suspended from school for using mouthwash after lunch; and a teacher fired for reprimanding an unruly student, only worsened his condition.

Common Sense lost ground when parents attacked teachers for doing the job that they themselves had failed to do in disciplining their unruly children. It declined even further when schools were required to get parental consent to administer sun lotion or an aspirin to a student, but were allowed to hand out free condoms without permission from parents.

Common Sense lost the will to live as the churches became businesses; and criminals received better treatment than their victims.

Common Sense took a beating when you couldn't defend yourself from a burglar in your own home and the burglar could sue you for assault.

Common Sense finally gave up the will to live, after a woman failed to realize that a steaming cup of coffee was hot. She spilled a little in her lap, and was promptly awarded a huge settlement.

Common Sense was preceded in death,
- by his parents, Truth and Trust,
- by his wife, Discretion,
- by his daughter, Responsibility,
- and by his son, Reason.

He is survived by his five stepbrothers;
- I Know My Rights
- I Want It Now
- Someone Else Is To Blame
- I'm A Victim
- Pay me for Doing Nothing

And his rich uncle in politics, Take the Money and Run

Not many attended his funeral because so few realized he was gone. If you still remember him, pass this on. If not, join the majority and do nothing. ~ Author Unknown

154

Legends of Masamune and Muramasa

A legend tells of a test where Muramasa challenged his master, Masamune, to see who could make a finer sword. They both worked tirelessly and eventually, when both swords were finished, they decided to test the results. The contest was for each to suspend the blades in a small creek with the cutting edge facing the current. Muramasa's sword, the Juuchi Yosamu cut everything that passed its way; fish, leaves floating down the river, the very air which blew on it. Highly impressed with his pupil's work, Masamune lowered his sword, the Yawarakai-Te, into the current and waited patiently. Not a leaf was cut, the fish swam right up to it, and the air hissed as it gently blew by the blade. After a while, Muramasa began to scoff at his master for his apparent lack of skill in the making of his sword. Smiling to himself, Masamune pulled up his sword, dried it, and sheathed it. All the while, Muramasa was heckling him for his sword's inability to cut anything. A monk, who had been watching the whole ordeal, walked over and bowed low to the two sword masters. He then began to explain what he had seen.

"The first of the swords was by all accounts a fine sword, however it is a blood thirsty, evil blade, as it does not discriminate as to who or what it will cut. It may just as well be cutting down butterflies as severing heads. The second was by far the finer of the two, as it does not needlessly cut that which is innocent and undeserving."

In another account of the story, both blades cut the leaves that went down on the river's current equally well, but the leaves would stick to the blade of Muramasa whereas they would slip on past Masamune's after being sliced. Or alternatively both leaves were cut, but those cut by Masamune's blade would reform as it traveled down the stream. Yet another version has leaves being sliced by Muramasa's blade while the leaves were repelled by Masamune's, and another again has leaves being sliced by Muramasa's blade and healed by Masamune's.
~Author Unknown

155

Drive

When the gazelle is being chased by a lion he runs his fastest to the point to where the heart will stop. Given maximum potential. When he no longer is being chased he will not run. He will walk idly by. Never pushing himself to his potential. What happens when there is no lion? What happens when there is not drive? Will you push yourself to the max without a driving force? The drive for a gazelle is not being eaten. What is your drive? What will stop you from being eaten?
~Author Unknown

156

The Two Farmers

There are two farmers in the field that are experiencing a drought. The worst drought they have seen in history. Every day after the work is done they sit down and pray for rain to water their crops. The rain never comes. The farmers continue to pray and pray but still to no avail. Both farmers continue to pray but one farmer starts to collect all the spare water jugs. Starts to dig out all the irrigation ditches to let the water through. The other farmer continues to laugh and call names at the farmer working. "Why are you doing this when there is no rain? It has not rained in months and all our crops will die, you are wasting your energy." The other farmer stops and looks upon his lifelong friend. You are foolish for not preparing for rain. We pray every day that God will bring rain. Until today neither one of us have prepared for when the rain comes. Right now God is testing is. God will bring the rain but are you prepared for it?

~Author Unknown

157

Warriors

There are two Native Americans that constantly train and pray to the war Gods for battle. Only one wakes up every morning and sharpens his knife. Oils his tomahawk, and makes more arrows. He never uses any of his war gear for day to day activity. The other Indian laughs at him, and tells him it is pointless to sharpen a knife that holds an edge sharp enough to shave with. Why do you oil your tomahawk when you have not used it? There is a whole area filled with arrows. We do not need anymore. Brother we train every day for battle, we pray every second for war. The God of war will bring us an enemy, but are you prepared for it?

~ Author Unknown

158

The Real Meaning of Peace

There once was a king who offered a prize to the artist who would paint the best picture of peace. Many artists tried. The king looked at all the pictures. But there were only two he really liked, and he had to choose between them.

One picture was of a calm lake. The lake was a perfect mirror for peaceful towering mountains all around it. Overhead was a blue sky with fluffy white clouds.

All who saw this picture thought it was a perfect picture of peace.

The other picture had mountains, too. But these were rugged and bare. Above was an angry sky, from which rain fell and in which lightning played. Down the side of the mountain tumbled a foaming waterfall. This did not look peaceful at all.

But when the king looked closely, he saw behind the waterfall a tiny bush growing in a crack in the rock. In the bush a mother bird had built her next. There, in the midst of the rush of angry water, sat the mother bird on her next – in perfect peace.

Which picture do you think won the prize? The king chose the second picture. Do you know why?

"Because" explained the king, "peace does not mean to be in a place where there is no noise, trouble, or hard work. Peace means to be in the midst of all those things and still be calm in your heart. That is the real meaning of peace." ~ Author Unknown

159

Keeping a Positive Attitude

Many people go through one point in their life where they feel defeated; they automatically say that "I can't do something." Sometimes even before attempting.

Edward Stewart Jr. had finally turned 13 years old. His life was constantly changing. In his mind, he was a hop-and-skip away from being an adult. Soon he would be getting his permit and driving. Junior reached into his pockets and saw that it was bare.

Junior decides to sit down and talk to his dad about receiving an allowance. He works all night and makes a makeshift presentation on why he deserves a stipend each week. Fifteen dollars was what he was hoping for. Sunday after church would be the day to have this man-to-man discussion. Junior sits and begins to lay out for his father his reasons for deserving an allowance. "Dad, I'm 13 now. I do my chores and I keep up my grades and I take care of my siblings. I'm the oldest and I take on the most responsibilities and I deserve to be rewarded with at least $15.00 a week for the things I do. What do you say to that?" Junior says.

His dad chuckles and looks down at the nice presentation his son created and reflects on the points made. "Sure thing, Junior. I think that you work hard around the house. You are growing into a fine young man.

If you truly want to show me that you deserve this allowance, then I have a proposition for you, son."

"Okay Dad, whatever it is you got it." Jimmy replies. "You know that we are expanding on the house, I just need your help with moving some supplies. I'll need roughly about an hour's work on Saturday. Are you up to it?" Junior's Dad asks.

"That's all I have to do and I will get an allowance? That's the easiest thing in the world. I worked that one summer cutting grass all day long. No matter what it is, I can do it!" Junior exclaimed.

The deal was set with the handshake between father and son.

Monday rolls around and Junior decides to ask out the prettiest girl in his class to the movies. She accepts. Junior is already spending this $15.00 because he knows in his mind and heart that he has it made already. For the rest of the week, Junior is planning the next 6 weeks of what he is going to do because he knows that this allowance is in his pocket.

Saturday morning rolls around and Junior jumps out of bed and instantly into his work overalls. He rushes down stairs and sits at the table. His mom knows how important this day is for her son and his task at hand so she made him pancakes, bacon, biscuits, and eggs. Junior eats his meal in record time and heads outside to his father who is currently gathering his tools and supplies in the front yard. His father greets him and begins walking Junior to the back of the house.

"Son, I know that you are ready to receive this allowance and I know that you are going to work hard to get it. As a part of our deal, I just need you to get something done for me in the hour." "Yes, Sir, I will get it done," he replies.

They finally arrive to the back yard, where there is a pallet of cinder blocks. "Well Son, I need you to move these cinder blocks from the back yard to the front, next to the driveway."

Junior's eyes look at the huge mountain of cinder blocks.

"Yes…Sir. I will try and move as much as I can in the hour." "No son, these are 32 cinder blocks that I need in the front of the yard in a hour. It's 9 o'clock on the dot. Do we still have a deal?" "Yes Sir, we do"

They both sync their watches and set the alarm for 10:00. His father turns and heads to the front yard, where he begins preparing the cement and leveling out the ground.

Junior stares at the cinder blocks, the obstacle standing in front of him was the only thing keeping him from getting his allowance. Junior reaches for the first cinder block and it feels like it weighs a ton. Junior moves the cinder block maybe 3 feet from the original pile and stops. "This is impossible. There has to be an easier way," he says.

Junior begins to look around the yard for his old sled. He decided that he would use his sled to pull the cinder blocks. Junior finally finds the sled but notices it's rotted from being outside in the elements. Junior heads back to the mountain of cinder blocks. "There is no way possible that I can do this in an hour. Dad set me up for failure." And with that, Junior sat on the first cinder block he originally tried to move and began kicking the dirt and throwing rocks at the huge pile of cinderblocks. Junior looks down at his watch: "9:05" it reads. He continues to sit there. Ten more minutes pass. Then ten more minutes pass: "9:25" his watch read. "Man I only have 35 more minutes...there is no way I can do this." Junior says as he hangs his head down.

Junior's father finally completed his task in preparing the cement and also leveling the area. He decides to go and check on his son's progress. His dad wipes away the sweat from his face and heads to the back yard. To his surprise he sees Junior playing with rocks, acting as though he had no care in his world. The piles of cinder were untouched besides the one cinder block Junior was sitting on. His dad begins to walk towards him. "Junior get up!" Junior immediately rises to his feet caught off guard. "What are you doing son? You haven't even moved one cinder block to the front."

"But Dad, this was impossible. These blocks weigh a ton and there are so many and it's just me moving them. I couldn't do it in an hour."

"Son, you didn't even try. I'm disappointed in your actions. You approached me like a man and agreed to this task and you didn't even attempt to try to accomplish it. You bear our last name. You are a Stewart and we don't think of quitting and we don't accept quitting either. I would have been happier if you moved those blocks for an hour straight, even if you didn't make the time hack but at least you would have tried. You have 30 minutes to work. I don't want to see you stop until I get back. Do you understand me?" "Yes Sir, I do," he replies.

Junior's dad leaves to go back to the front to continue to prep the work area. Junior feels so low at this point. His dad was right. Not only did Junior not attempt his task but he let his father down by not trying. So Junior decided he would move as many blocks as he could in the last 30 minutes. Junior grabs 2 cinder blocks and begins to walk to the front yard; it takes him 2 minutes. He grabs two more, and then 2 more. Junior looks down at his watch…he is truly racing against time. There is only 10 minutes left until his deadline, with 14 cinder blocks left. He grabs 2 and goes as quickly as he can; 2 more and then 2 more…and 2 more. Junior is starting to feel fatigue set in but he continues to push through. Junior is finally down to the last 2 cinder blocks but he has 45 seconds until the end of his time allotted. Junior picks the cinder blocks up and begins to move them as quickly as he can. He gets about half way to the front when his alarm on his watch goes off and with that Junior's heart sinks. He was close to finishing his task, even after starting 25 minutes late. He drops the cinder blocks and sits down on one of them. His head hanging low, he hears his father walk up to him and then takes a seat on the other cinder block beside him.

"Son, look at what you were able to accomplish in such a short time. Imagine what you would have done if you had the entire time and worked hard from the very start." "I would have finished my task. I know I disappointed you Dad" he says.

"What I need you to understand Junior is that if you tell yourself that you can't do something, you won't. If you defeat yourself mentally, the task will be the size of a mountain. This is a lesson I want you to always keep with you. No matter what you do in this life, always go in with a positive mindset. Can you do that for me Son?" "Yes Sir. I will." Junior's dad pats his son on the back and together they took the two final blocks to the front yard.

~ Lawanda Ruiz

Index

Adversity: state of hardship or difficulty; misfortune; harsh conditions; hard times.

Appreciation: a positive emotion or attitude in acknowledgment of a benefit that one has received or will receive with no strings attached.

Character: the inherent complex of attributes that determines a person's moral and ethical actions and reactions in all situations. It's who you are when someone is not watching.

Commitment: accomplish any mission and personally and professionally being responsible for your actions.

Confidence: assurance: freedom from doubt; belief in yourself and your abilities that you can do anything.

Courage: in the face of intimidation and uncertainty, living your life with a warrior spirit around values, traits and principles, both morally and mentally.

Encouragement: the act of encouraging; incitement to action or to practice; as, the encouragement of being generous.

Faith: the confident belief or trust in the truth or trustworthiness of a person.

Friendship: is the cooperative and supportive relationship between people.

God Created All Men Equal: Thomas Jefferson borrowed the expression from an Italian friend and neighbor, Philip Mazzei, and used it in our Declaration of Independence.

Honor: living your life with integrity, responsibility, honesty and respect.

**Hope: is a belief in a positive outcome related to events
and circumstances in one's life. Hope is the feeling that
what is wanted can be had or that events will turn out
for the best.**

Humility: the quality of being humble: modest, not proud, doing something out of the goodness of your heart, not for yourself. It's not about you!

Mentoring: refers to a professional and/or personal developmental relationship in which a more experienced or more knowledgeable person helps a less experienced or less knowledgeable person 24/7/365; unconditionally.

Patience: is the state of endurance under all circumstances, which can mean persevering in the face of delay or provocation without acting on annoyance/anger in a negative way.

Joseph Shusko served as a Marine Corps Officer from 1975 until 2006. He is a lifelong athlete and student of mentoring and leadership principles. Shusko lives in Stafford, Virginia with his lovely lady Kadie.

Additional Reading

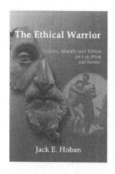

The Ethical Warrior
Jack Hoban was shaped by service in the U.S. Marine Corps, a life-changing epiphany at a Cold War bar, and mentorship under two masters. He now delivers a revolutionary view of moral values for our time epitomized by the Ethical Warrior – protector of self and others as equal human beings.

The Ethical Protector
Federal Agent Bruce Gourlie and RGI President Jack Hoban deliver this timely and timeless book adapted from a series of articles written originally for LEOs on PoliceOne.com. The book provides critical tactical insights, as well as, philosophical and psychological clarity for the protector in all of us – especially those who are "on the job."

Values Fort A New Millennium
Robert L. Humphrey was an Iwo Jima veteran, Harvard graduate, and cross cultural conflict resolution specialist during the Cold War. He proposed the "Dual Life Value Theory" of Human Nature, which can help us: Reduce Violence, Revitalize Our Schools, and Promote Cross-Cultural Harmony.

Available at: www.rgi.co/ethicalwarriorbook/

Made in the USA
Middletown, DE
08 July 2015